Kristie
I am so Godly
proud of you!
You are blossoming into
an amazing woman of God!
Keep going + growing!
Love

unfold through the
revelation in this book
and the engaging times
you experience in the
Spirit! Thank you for
your support!
Melanie

The Anatomy of The Courts: An Introduction to the Government of Heaven

By Kingdom Culture, Inc.

Kristie
B-E-A-U-TI-FUL
Your so gorgeous and I'm
so glad we're connected!!
I can't wait to see who
God blossoms you into!!
Be Blessed

Kristie,
I love you so very much
and you are finally
coming to see how glorious
and beautiful you truly
are. May you grow in
this revelation more
and more and
be filled All the
way up in God's
love and power and
His plan for you!
Love, Alysha Reddy

Printed in the United States of America

First Printing, 2018

ISBN 978-164370978-9

Kingdom Culture, Inc.
www.kingdomcultureinc.org

Contributing Authors and Illustrators:
Anita Logan
Melanie Moore
Aleshia Redding
Wendi Richardson
Belinda Jackson

Book cover designed by:
The Mind Box Design & Marketing Firm, LLC
Atlanta, GA
www.themindbox.com

Scripture quotations in this publication appear from the following Bible versions:

King James Version
The Message Version
New American Standard Bible
New International Version
New King James Version
New Living Translation

Dedication

This book is dedicated to our beautiful "Nauna", who was the catalyst that started it all. The following are the words of her mother and the sentiments of all of our hearts.

Bryauna Michele Richardson
1999 - 2011
(Earthly Birth) (Heavenly Graduation)

The eight days before you transitioned from here to Heaven taught me more than I thought I was capable of learning. I never knew I could love so deeply and I had no idea what was in store. All I knew was that I trusted God and I still do. He asked me for my "Isaac seed" then He gave me Heaven. This is dedicated to you Nauna. Your faith has been my fuel.

I still believe,
Mommy

Acknowledgements

We want to give loving honor and thanks to the Godhead – Father, Jesus, and Holy Spirit – You are our reason for being and the One we love. Thank you for giving us the honor of co-laboring with You!

Thanks to our families: the Logan Family, the Moore Family, and the Redding Family. Thank you for all of your love, prayer and support. We wouldn't be who we are without you.

Thank you Pastor Samuel & Pastor Ayanna Giles, Tonthallel Walters, and Andrea Randall. Your tireless effort and guidance have been invaluable. We could not have done this without you!

Thanks to the entire KCI family for all of your patience, support and commitment. We are KCI and KCI is US!! We love you all!

Table of Contents

Foreword

For all of humanity, Jesus Christ became the standard for how man was to live in communion with the Father and administrate His Kingdom on the earth. When we examine His life, especially His development, we see hidden keys that demonstrate the process for becoming a Son of God. Like many of us, Jesus was born into a peculiar situation and suffered the ridicule of many based on the origin of His existence. Yet as we look at what we know about His development, He survived murder attempts, slander, skepticism, and ridicule all while becoming the model of the perfect man. The bible indicates in Luke 2:40 of Jesus that in His most formative years of development in the natural, He also grew in the Spirit, "***40*** *And the Child grew and became strong in spirit, filled with wisdom; and the grace of God was upon Him.*" Jesus then put to use what He had been given access to and by means of use, confounded the teachers in the synagogue at the age of 12. The scriptures tell us that He then grew stronger and matured into His next level as He grew in stature and in favor with God and man. In His adulthood, we see that Jesus demonstrated His dominion in the earth through miracles, signs and wonders. He Co-labored with the Father by only doing what He saw His Father do and Governed from His seat of Authority as all of creation, angels, demons, even the winds and waves obeyed His voice.

For every believer that comes into the knowledge of the Lord Jesus Christ as their personal Savior, there is an expected growth pattern that is initiated as soon as the heart believes and confession is made unto salvation. And in each phase of that growth pattern the Lord has established key principles and measurement points (milestones), which indicate the person's maturation and ability to handle the responsibilities that come at each level. In the natural we are born into the earth as infant babes that cannot survive and properly develop in the new tumultuous environment called earth, without the diligent nurture and loving care of someone that has been entrusted with our development. Like infants growing into adolescence, what we learn during these most formative years of our development will dictate the degree of functionality that we will have as teenagers, young adults and into adulthood. The proper combination of dietary nourishment, loving family, and mental stimulation creates the best environment needed to sustain healthy growth.

And while many people will agree with my cursory (rudimentary) assessment of the natural development process of a person into adulthood, unfortunately, not as many would readily agree that their spiritual development followed the same pattern. There is a desperate condition of arrested development suffered by many in body of Christ because the same care that is seen as normal and necessary in the natural was not applied to their spiritual development. This condition has left many malnourished and under developed, still clinging onto the elementary things of the faith. The most egregious thing is that although in the natural there are laws that enforce harsh consequences and raise a public outcry for negligence in the care or delinquency of a minor, the same is not in place for the gross negligence that can be seen in the spiritual development of far too many in the Body of Christ.

This has left many in the Body of Christ in cycles of sin and complacency while others are crying out saying “There Has to Be More to God than this.” What I love about the Father is that the cry of His people always gets His attention. And He will find someone willing to receive revelation from Him to spark revival and bring spiritual nourishment to the lives of the hungry. In the richness of His Mercy, He will use that same revelation to rebuke the complacent of their lethargy and provoke them to hunger after maturation and their rightful position as sons of God. 1 Corinthians 3:1-16 and Hebrew 5:12-15 are examples of that rebuke and provocation.

The Anatomy of the Courts of Heaven as well as the journey of KCI was born out of the cry of 4 young ladies who said that “There Has to be More.” Though their life circumstances were not ideal by any means, it was these insurmountable circumstances that provoked in them a pursuit of the Lord that welcomed them into a lifestyle of knowing their identities in

Christ. It is from this place that they have chosen to possess their promised inheritance to rule and reign with Him.

This book is filled with fundamental truths that are key to every believer knowing who they are in Christ, the position that they have in Him, and the standard they need to live by to maintain that position. You will be masterfully taken on a journey to know what the covenantal rights of sonship are as you are introduced to the Government of Heaven, the Kingdom of Heaven, and the Holy Spirit, who ushers you into a life in the supernatural. You will learn how to work in concert with the agenda of Heaven and glean from the lives of some of the great men and women of God who readily lived in this dimension of heavenly activity. Lastly, in the Anatomy of the Courts of Heaven section you will learn that the Courts are a real place in Heaven that the Righteous Judge and King issues judgments and decrees from. You will learn the nature of the legal proceedings and most importantly the role you play as a son and Kingdom Ambassador in getting those judgments issued to live a victorious life according to the will of the Father.

The Anatomy of the Courts is a game changer for every believer. Whether you are newly saved or have been walking with the Lord for a while, I believe that your diligent examination of this book will accelerate your growth in God, as well as position you to govern with Him. This book will train you to be prepared to engage the Kingdom of Heaven to get the blueprints to dismantle demonic strongholds in your life. Buckle your seatbelts and get ready to have your life transformed as you live out the principles spelled out in this book by Anita, Aleshia, Melanie, and Wendi that transformed their lives. May you be fully engulfed by the reality of Heaven's Courts and the one who sits upon the throne, the King of Glory, the Righteous Judge, The Lord of Hosts.

Pastor Samuel O. Giles Jr.

Introduction

The textbook you are about to read is a miracle. Not even four years ago we were each on our own individual journeys in God. Some of us had not even met yet, and we certainly did not share the same relationships we enjoy with one another now. We are different ages with different backgrounds and different life experiences. But, unbeknownst to us, there was one major common trait that drew us, and in a way, binds us. Each of us cried to God from the depths of our beings, "GOD THERE MUST BE MORE THAN THIS!"

We were each desperate for more than what we'd been taught. We wanted more than what we had experienced of God up to that point in our lives. We needed answers for tragedies we faced and an understanding of the drive to go deeper, but had no one to show us how.

Now, four years later, here we are. We have the privilege of sharing with you the beginning of God's response to our hearts' cry. This book is about displaying the truth of the Kingdom and the heart of God in such a way that you, too, can get answers about who are, why you are here and what God has in store for your amazing life. Our prayer is that the power of the transformation God has brought into our lives through this revelation of the Government of Heaven becomes active in your life as you journey with us through these pages. Let the journey begin!

Section I: Dominion

Chapter 1: Introduction to the Government of Heaven

The Government of Heaven cannot be adequately discussed without first looking at the concept of DOMINION. When God created man, He not only created us to be in relationship with Him but we were also created to rule and reign with Him. God created us to have a major role and position in His government, which we refer to as the Government of Heaven. It is this specific GOVERNMENT that is designed to rule both the HEAVENS and the EARTH.

It was prophesied at the birth of Jesus that *"...the government shall be upon His shoulders and to the increase of His government there shall be no end."* This let's us know that Jesus is the head of the government of Heaven and has the responsibility of making sure it's carried out. However, the government is to be carried on the, SHOULDERS of Christ. The last I checked, the shoulders were apart of the body, and who is the body... we are! Therefore that means that you and I, as apart of the body of Christ, were designed to help establish the Government of Heaven in the earth.

No matter how evil and perverse the world may be, Heaven's governmental system is more powerful than it has ever been! It is not weakening or dwindling, In fact the scripture says that His Government will never stop increasing. This means we will never be out of work. It's our responsibility to ensure the dominion of Heaven permeates the entire earth through the authority God gave us.

Therefore, when Jesus began to teach the disciples in the New Testament concerning prayer and standing in the gap, He told them to pray this: Matt. 6:10 "*Thy kingdom come. Thy will be done in earth, as [it is] in heaven.*" (Matthew 6:10) This is one of the major prayer assignments that Jesus gave to us: to intercede so that Heaven can overtake the earth. This task is left up to us!

The government of God was first introduced in Genesis, when man was created in the earth. God gave us an assignment to rule and govern when He told man to "*... subdue it, and have dominion over the fish of the sea, and over the fowl of the air, and over every living thing that moveth upon the earth.*" (Gen. 1:28)

This is when we were first given the authority to have dominion over the earth as His children. Webster's dictionary defines Dominion as Law, supreme authority over a land. This definition also aligns with the biblical concept. The Hebrew word for Dominion in Genesis is Radah: rule, prevailed, subdue.

Psalm 115:16 confirms this "*The heavens are the Lord's heavens, but the earth he has given to the children of man.*" So, when God gave us Dominion, he intended for us to rule, to have authority over the earthly realm. This includes the earth and its atmosphere. Adam and Eve were tasked with establishing heaven's government in the kingdom of the earth through ruling and governing, i.e. by having DOMINION. "*Thou madest him to have dominion over the works of thy hands; thou hast put all things under his feet:*" (Psalm 8:6)

When we look at the term 'rule', it simply means to exercise authority over. However, the concept of dominion governing takes it a step further. The word dominion not only means to rule but it means to exercise continuous sovereign rule and authority in a specific territory or land. So, to sum it up, the concept of dominion in this context is a continuous state of Godly ruling and governing. When a kingdom or government overtakes a territory, it exercises continual domination. This level of dominion is accomplished by establishing the laws and the customs of the conquering Kingdom throughout the entire land.

For example, when Great Britain conquered land anywhere in the world, (as they did in Africa) their ambassadors were sent to train the people of that land in the ways of the British government and culture. The environment and society was transformed to operate like the government of their homeland, England. This transformation would begin at the point of the SMALLEST detail of their English custom of teatime three-four times each day. As they conquered each territory, the people in that land were required to implement the English language, laws, religion and yes, even tea times. These implementations were required to establish the new regime (their governmental systems) of the new kingdom that has taken control.

THIS scenario gives us a very small example of what true dominion looks like. This was God's intention when we were instructed to have dominion in the earth. When God gave man this task, He intended for us to establish continuous sovereignty and authority from God into the earth. What does that look like, right? Essentially, what this means is that the world sounds like, looks like and operates like HEAVEN. More specifically, society and culture would be operating under Heaven's laws, its language, its supernatural power, its wealth, its culture of honor, and especially the habitation of God' s glory and tangible presence.

It's one thing to conquer new territory and make a few adjustments in its governmental structure. However, the word dominion (and God's intent behind it) indicates a complete and total take over as if the other never existed. As it pertains to the dominion given to man, the entire earth is set for a transformation to be taken out of the influence of darkness and baptized into the operation of the Kingdom of Heaven.

One of Jesus' assignments when he came to the earth was to prepare men to assume their role of establishing Heaven's dominion on earth. He told the disciples in Matthew 10: 7-8 "*And as ye go, preach, saying, the kingdom of heaven is at hand. Heal the sick, cleanse the lepers, raise the dead, cast out devils: freely ye have received, freely give.*" In other words, go tell everybody that the Kingdom of Heaven is here and is operating to clean up all satanic rule of perversion. The Kingdom is here to reverse the damage and scars of demonic influences that have ruled the land and the people in the land for thousands of years.

So, let's connect some dots and lay a bit more foundation.

Before man came on the scene in the earth, God already existed, and Heaven, His dwelling place, was already functioning in full capacity. Things were peaceful, beautiful, all together lovely and pure perfection. The streets were already paved with gold and the river of life was flowing throughout the city. There was no need for the sun because the light of God was (and still is) the brightness of the city.

Let me paint a picture for you, imagine this: The enemy, lucifer, was the covering cherubim and one of the Arc angels along with Michael (Head of the Hosts – Warrior Angels) and Gabriel (Head of the Messenger Angels). Angels were appointed to sing, worship, and create, all while living in the best place anyone could ever dream. Life was great without a worry or a care.

At this point, there was no need for Michael's Warfare Department because there were no opposing forces. Then one day, lucifer had this thought in his heart. "…I *will ascend into heaven, I will exalt my throne above the stars of God: I will sit also upon the mount of the congregation, in the sides of the north: I will ascend above the heights of the clouds; I will be like the most High.*" (Isaiah 14: 13-14)

He begins to entertain this thought and began putting it into action. He persuaded one-third of the angels to side with him. As a result, he was kicked out of Heaven with one-third of the angels that he persuaded. I'm not sure how he deceived a third of the angels to side against God. All of these angels had direct access to God and His powerful presence. Yet, somehow, they were still deceived and kicked out of Heaven along with lucifer.

Now in a state of exile, I can imagine that satan was furious and at his wits end. What was satan really going to do? The enemy knew he could not do anything against God himself. We must remember that satan is NOT, I repeat NOT God's equal in any way shape or form. God created lucifer; so actually, the enemy was one of God's original creations. The enemy cannot do anything against God himself. However, the way satan tries to get back at God is by harming or even destroying what's near and dear to God's heart… Mankind!

When we really think about it, man arrived fashionably late to the party. There was already a 'war' going on. The enemy was in a fight to have dominion wherever he could. Then, here comes one of the enemy's worst nightmares… MAN! Mankind was given the authority and power over this earthly realm that satan thought belonged to him. Not only was/is satan jealous of man, but I'm sure this made him more furious to see how endearing God was toward man to give him this level of authority. When God created man, He gave man the power and authority to rule and have dominion in the earth. God stepped into time and said, "*Let us make man in our image…*" God gave man His image, His likeness, even His breath, making him a living soul with the privilege of making choices. Man is God's heartthrob. Man has been God's greatest joy and greatest heartbreak since the beginning. Nothing and no one causes God's heart to turn and in the same instance be filled with love and compassion like mankind.

The love God has for us is indescribable and surrounds us wherever we go. Paul wrote:

"*For I am persuaded, that neither death, nor life, nor angels, nor principalities, nor powers, nor things present, nor things to come, nor height, nor depth, nor any other creature, shall be able to separate us from the love of God, which is in Christ Jesus our Lord.*"
Romans 8:38 - 39

David wrote a psalm that exemplifies how deep and how unwavering God's love is for us; no matter where we are, He and His love are there. He wrote... "...*Even if I make my bed in hell, thou art with me...*" (Psalm 139:8) Wow, that is powerful. God is slow to anger and faithful to forgive. After God delivers our ancestors, the children of Israel, from Egypt, He expresses how much He still loves and cherishes them. Exodus 19:4-5 reads "...*how I bare you on eagles' wings, and brought you unto myself. Now therefore, if ye will obey my voice indeed, and keep my covenant, then ye shall be a peculiar treasure unto me above all people...*" And to top it all off, "...H*e gave his only son...*" (John 3:16) because of the LOVE he has for us.

Even with God's omniscience (all knowing abilities), He knew the roads we would take. Yet He still made us in His own image, called us sons and positioned us as royalty to rule and reign with Him. God designed MAN to be a part of the Dominion plan in the earth to co-labor and co-partner with Him as sons; His cherished family.

At this point, I can imagine satan squirming and "hustlin'" to devise a plan of destruction to take this authority from man. Although satan's original plan was to create a throne above God's (hahahahaha, right, not even...that's hilarity), he had no choice but to go after the dominion of earth instead. Since the fall of man, satan became the arch enemy, opposing all of God's Kingdom.

HOW DID THE EARTH BECOME SO DAMAGED IF WE HAVE BEEN GIVEN DOMINION?

After the fall of Adam, satan assumed the power and authority over the earth, This would include the world and its atmosphere would be set in a direction of evil and demonic dominance. As previously stated, dominion and authority were given to man to rule over the earth. This included the atmosphere that surrounds the earth. Man was once in full authority, until Adam and Eve ate of the tree of the knowledge of good and evil. In their disobedience (Genesis 3: 5-7) man forfeited their access to God. This is when the enemy took authority over the earth and the earthly realm by default. After the fall of man, our access to God drastically changed and man was kicked out of the garden.

However, the enemy is deemed to be the prince of the air because we gave up our place in the Garden. "*Wherein in time past ye walked according to the course of this world, according to the prince of the power of the air, the spirit that now worketh in the children of disobedience:*" (Ephesians 2:2) This is the very reason why maturing as sons of God is so vitally important so that we can stand in the authority Jesus took back with the finished works of the cross.

The key thing to remember is when man was kicked out of the Garden of Eden; they no longer had DIRECT access to God. The loss of this access caused the wall of separation to get stronger, louder and taller. Adam and Eve were kicked out of God's garden and stripped of their physical, tangible connection with God. At this point, they were no longer ONE with God. The iniquities and appetite of the flesh that were ignited as a result of the fall, made it extremely difficult and almost impossible for man to fulfill the dominion assignment until Jesus came to earth.

Man now had to toil and eat by the work of his hands and the sweat of his brow. Whereas, before the fall, the pulse of God's energy caused effortless and insurmountable work to be done with ease. The corrupt DNA allowed the flesh to become a dominant factor in the life of mankind. As the flesh became the dominant factor it created enmity between man and God, rendering us powerless against the devices of the enemy. (Man's spirit grew weaker and the enmity between God and man grew stronger as time passed from man's eviction out of the garden.)

Let's look at the meaning of enmity: The word enmity indicates hostility, separation, war, a divide between two entities. As we journey through the scriptures, we see this term enmity is connected to our flesh and it builds a divide between God and us. "*Because the carnal mind is enmity against God: for it is not subject to the law of God, neither indeed can be. So, then they that are in the flesh cannot please God* (Romans 8: 7-8). However, Ephesians confirms that Jesus tore down this wall of division, reconciling us back to God, giving us DIRECT access again to our Father through Jesus.

"But now in Christ Jesus ye who sometimes were far off are made nigh by the blood of Christ. For he is our peace, who hath made both one, and hath broken down the middle wall of partition between us; Having abolished in his flesh the enmity, even the law of commandments contained in ordinances; for to make in himself of twain one new man, so making peace; And that he might reconcile both unto God in one body by the cross, having slain the enmity thereby:" Ephesians 2:14-16

Since mankind was created, we were designed to have dual citizenship in both Heaven and in the earth with Heaven being our base. From the beginning, it was God's intent to give us legal rights and authority, through dominion, over the earth and the earthly realm. Adam and Eve lived in the garden, which was God's garden as referenced in Ezekiel 28: 13. The garden was a bridge or connector between Heaven and earth; a doorway or access point that allowed man to go back and forth. When Adam and Eve sinned, that entry point was closed and guarded from man (Genesis 3: 23 - 24). As time progressed, God created other portals in the earthly realm for us to have a small measure of access to Heaven. We see this with the pool of Bethesda when an angel would come once a year to touch the water and people were healed.

"For an angel went down at a certain season into the pool, and troubled the water: whosoever then first after the troubling of the water stepped in was made whole of whatsoever disease he had." John 5:4

We also saw this when only the High Priest could enter into the Holy of Holies. It was actually a direct supernatural portal or access to God in Heaven. This is also seen in the case of Jacob's ladder where angels descended and ascended back and forth from Heaven to earth. However, the crucifixion of Jesus reversed everything and it all changed: the HEAVENS WERE OPENED to us, and we were granted ACCESS back to the Father, back to our Heavenly home once again.

During the time that enmity was present, the voice or word of God would come from a prophet, or designated man or woman of God or through dreams and visions. This was why the Prophets were so major during this time. The Prophets were the few who heard God directly when most people could not. Man no longer walked in God's garden in the cool of the day to get impartations of His mysteries, wisdom and power. When man would directly walk with the presence of God in the garden everyday, a strong bond of love and oneness would be formed. Man's oneness with God was AND STILL IS the flow from which comes the most potent levels of power.

This was AND STILL IS the flow of the most potent levels of power in the Lord; being one with God. Jesus died, to destroy that wall of separation between God and man, to restore our oneness with Him again. *"For through him we both have access by one Spirit unto the Father."* (Ephesians 2:18) Our oneness with God gives us access to the fullness of His presence and UNLIMITED access to the power of our God. This empowers us to take our rightful place as sons and heirs. It is this positioning that establishes our dominion in the earth so that Heaven's Government can reign supreme through us and in the earth.

With the fall of mankind, satan thought his alternate goal would finally came through. Then enemy knew he could not defeat God, he was going to do everything he could to be like God and have his throne over the stars. Because man was separated from God, satan assumed that man's flesh was too weak to come against his works. He knew any surge of power from man would be temporary. The enemy took comfort in knowing the strength of man could not pierce the expanding, thick exterior of darkness created to enthrone him as prince and establish his dominion of darkness.

However, what the enemy didn't realize was the fullness of who Jesus really was. *"For in him dwelleth all the fulness of the Godhead bodily and ye are complete in him, which is the head of all principality and power: " (*Colossians 2:9-10) Jesus came and took the keys to death, hell and the grave. The enemy was defeated and dethroned through the finished works of the cross. He came to reestablish us in our rightful place as sons, heirs and rulers of the earth with Christ.

We've heard about healings, miracles and supernatural occurrences that are truly a part of the Kingdom of Heaven. However, these events are limited when Heaven's Government (it's laws, its systems and operations) is not reigning on the earth. Heaven's Government is established when we begin to walk in total dominion in the earth.

When Heaven's Government is established: sickness, poverty, confusion, and/or bondage will cease to exist. When Heaven's policies and operations are finally established in the earth through, these things like sickness, etc. cannot exist because they are apart of the satanic government that won't be able to prevail. All activity contrary to Heaven's dominion cannot stand under the weight of God's glory and presence! How do we know this? Before the fall of Adam and Eve, there was NO sickness, no lack or poverty, no toil, no confusion and no bondage! When man was in his rightful place of sonship and dominion, the Kingdom of Heaven and its government had total dominance and the enemy could not prevail. However, BECAUSE of the fall, the curse of sin entered the domain of the earth.

"*Thorns also and thistles shall it bring forth to thee; and thou shalt eat the herb of the field; In the sweat of thy face shalt thou eat bread, till thou return unto the ground; for out of it wast thou taken: for dust thou art, and unto dust shalt thou return.*" Genesis 1:18-19

Before the fall, there was no death, no working by the sweat of our brow and no tilling of the ground. However, when sin took place, it opened the door for the enemy's domain to come into the earth and reign. Please note, when we sin, or when sin remains in our bloodline, it opens the door for satan to bring curses and turmoil. The enemy is doing his best to reverse the original plan and order God set forth in the earth. His plan is to make you fall and lose connection with God. Through the mediums of society, he (satan) methodically seduced generations to live their lives outside of the Dominion of God and has caused a mass reproduction of an untoward generation.

Each generation steps further and further away from the realm of God causing ignorance and distance to strengthen with each decade. The enemy's influence can easily be seen in the chaos of hurricanes, the trauma of mass shootings, or even the pains of homelessness and poverty. However, the separation between God and man had the greatest deception on humanity. Not realizing who God is, and not knowing who we are keeps us from understanding that WE were created to reign WITH Him. God has given us Dominion to guard against the weapons and the tyranny of the enemy. The biggest deception of all is not realizing the importance of connecting to our Father, His throne and His home for us in Heaven.

When God gave man the commandment to have Dominion, the earth was already in compliance with God's laws. Adam and Eve were created in a world where the stage of Heaven's domain was already set. Man was put in place to govern and have Dominion over the atmosphere that was already under His ruling.

THE MOMENT Adam and Eve fell, the enemy took full advantage of the lost authority (in the garden) and the fight was ON. The Fight for what? The Fight for DOMINION and who will have authority over the earth! When we receive Christ, we become joint-heirs with Him. His blood paid the price for the sins that kept us from our rightful place of authority with him; granting us access back to the Father by the Spirit through the blood of Christ. Our assignment was given thousands of years ago and it has NOT changed. It seemed almost impossible to carry out this assignment after the fall, but the cross was the game changer! After the cross, the way was made for us to carry out Matthew 6, with fervor. This scripture confirms our mandate to stand in the gap and make sure the structure, the laws, and the order of Heaven are established in the earth. We have the power of the Holy Ghost so we should now be UNSTOPPABLE!! Right??? So, what's stopping us??? (Selah)

CHAPTER 1 REVIEW QUESTIONS

1. What is the definition of Dominion?
2. Explain who is responsible for the government of Heaven being established in the earth? Please use scripture reference.
3. Please give examples in scripture of God's love for mankind
4. What caused the separation between God and man?
5. Please explain more of the impact that resulted from the fall of mankind?

Chapter 2: Kingdom of Heaven

Growing up as a preacher's kid, I remember hearing preachers, teachers and singers, refer to Heaven as this faraway place that we will experience after we die. Of course we would only go to Heaven if we were saved and lived a holy life before the Lord in this earth. Little did I realize that it was meant for all of God's children who were saved to access and experience Heaven while on the earth.

There has always been a great mysterious 'cloud' of ambiguity around the subject of Heaven. What is it like? What's really up there? Are we only bowing down worshipping for thousands of years when we get there? What will we really be doing up there? Many people, even some non-Christians, believe in Heaven's existence. Most even believe that it's a final destination with only happy days of peace and rest for those who accepted Jesus in their hearts and lived for God. However, understanding there is no more dying there, and that there is only blissfulness and sunny days, is not enough anymore. **IF WE ARE GOING TO BE CHANGE AGENTS** and vessels who will be bringing Heaven's invasion in earth, we have to begin expanding our knowledge and belief about our Home. We have now entered a season in the body of Christ where it's time to understand the functions and technologies about the Kingdom of Heaven.

Jesus constantly referred to himself as an 'alien', or someone who was not of this world. "*They are not of the world, even as I am not of the world*" (John 17:16). Yet He was sent to redeem the world and bring our hearts back into alignment with the reason we were positioned in this world. As He journeyed the land manifesting signs, wonders and miracles, Jesus told us "*Verily, verily, I say unto you, He that believeth on me, the works that I do shall he do also; and greater works than these shall he do;*" (John 14:12). So, if we are to be like Jesus, and operate like Jesus, then we must know Heaven as He does and engage in Heavenly realms even while we are on earth.

Heaven is THE MOST BEAUTIFUL, PERFECT, WONDERFUL, AMAZING, SERENE YET JOYOUS, RESTFUL, FUN, and GLORIOUS place that will ever exist. There are streets paved with pure gold and city gates of pearl with all the colors of the rainbow and more. There are beautiful creatures big and small and it is so unwaveringly bright with the light of our Father (Revelation 21:21-27).

Most importantly, Heaven is where our God lives and dwells. It is not only where he lives, but it IS his throne. "*Thus, saith the Lord, The* ***HEAVEN IS MY THRONE****, and the earth is my footstool...*" (Isaiah 66:1) From Heaven, God rules and reigns and His Spirit takes residence. This is where God takes council with the Godhead and decides what strategic moves to implement His plans for this world and our lives. He did the same in the garden when He said, "*Let us make man, in our likeness.*" (Genesis 1: 26) From Heaven flows the pure and perfect origination of the systems, technologies, and areas of influence found in the earth. Heaven is the origin of what we do and how we operate. Earth is only a slight glimpse of Heaven's operation and set up. In Job, God declares how it was HE who created the earth, and all methods and foundations originate with Him. "*Where were you when I created the earth? Tell me, since you know so much!"... Who decided on its size? Certainly, you would know that! Who came up with the blueprints and measurements? How was its foundation poured...*" (Job 38:4-6).

For so long, this world's view and influence has been so paramount in our lives that it blocked the prominence and reality of Heaven. Some believe that Heaven is important for 'someday when I die' or 'when the rapture happens'. However, many still fail to see the importance of engaging with Heaven while on earth. Some only think we can engage with Heaven as a place when we die; a final destination. However, Heaven is our home. It is where we originated in the thoughts of God. It is also the place that was re-opened for us to operate from when Jesus died on the cross. "*He took our sin-dead lives and made us alive in Christ. He did all this on his own, with no help from us! Then he picked us up and set us down in highest heaven in company with Jesus, our Messiah.*" (Ephesians 2:6 MSG). The plans of our lives are there in a scroll, a book created for us as a guide to accomplish God's will. The author in Psalm confirms that we all have a book with our specific destines; that contains every day, hour, minute and second of our lives. "*Then said I, Lo, I come: in the volume of the book it is written of me, I delight to do thy will, O my God: yea, thy law is within my heart.*" (Psalm 40:7-8)

In Heaven lies the essence of who we are. If we are negligent in engaging Heaven in our affairs, we will miss the will of the father. When we rightfully engage with Heaven, we can pray the will of our Father be manifested in the earth as it is in Heaven. In Matthew 6, Jesus was teaching the disciples about the basis and foundation of all prayer ..."*Thy kingdom come, Thy will be done in earth, as it is in heaven.*" (Matthew 6:10) Jesus gives clear directive on how we should pray God's will in earth, as it is lived out in HEAVEN.

When Jesus walked the earth and began to do mighty miracles, He told the masses He only does what He sees his Father do. "*Verily, verily, I say unto you, The Son can do nothing of himself, but what he seeth the Father do: for what things soever he doeth, these also doeth the Son likewise.*" (John 5:19) At this time Jesus was on the earth and His Father yet in Heaven. When Jesus talked about seeing what His Father does, I believe He had visual insight and actual access into the realm of Heaven to see what the Father was doing. Jesus is our example of bringing Heaven down to earth to do the Father's will. So, if we are following the instructive command of Jesus regarding praying that the Kingdom come to earth, we must understand more about what Heaven is, and how it operations.

Let's explore what the scriptures say about Heaven. Getting a better picture about Heaven can help us when we are praying for God's Kingdom to come and His will be done in the earth.

HEAVEN IS FULL OF LIFE

Heaven is a place, as mentioned before, where there is no death. It is also a place where sorrow and grief are washed away. We get a sneak peak of the environment of Heaven reading John's experience in Heaven. *"And God shall wipe away all tears from their eyes; and there shall be no more death, neither sorrow, nor crying, neither shall there be any more pain: for the former things are passed away."* (Rev. 21:4)

HEAVEN IS A SIN FREE ZONE

There is no sin, iniquity or practice of evil doing. The environment is sinless. Therefore, the effects, impact and wages of sin do not exist in Heaven. This is often hard for us to imagine because all our lives, sin has reigned in the earth. However, in Heaven there is no sin. The enemy was kicked out of Heaven because iniquity was found in him. "*Thou wast perfect in thy ways from the day that thou wast created, till iniquity was found in thee.*" (Ezekiel 28: 15). Heaven's laws and government establishes a sin free, iniquity free zone.

"*The Son of man shall send forth his angels, and they shall gather out of his kingdom all things that offend, and them which do iniquity;"* (Matt. 13:41).

HEAVEN IS WEALTHY

"*But my God shall supply all your need according to his riches in glory by Christ Jesus"* (Philippians 4:19). This scripture is actually referring to riches and wealth of Heaven. There is no lack, no poverty or disparity in Heaven. Our God owns the cattle on the thousand hills. All things belong to Him, including all the gold, all the silver and all the precious stones. From the beginning of the earth God provided riches from His Kingdom to the earth through Eden. In Eden, there was ONE river (the River of Life), which parted into four heads or sections, to water the garden in Eden. The first partition or section of that river was called Pison and it was full of gold, bdellium and onyx stone (Genesis 2:10-11). Eden was a representation of the wealth of Heaven.

HEAVEN REJOICES & CELEBRATES

One of the many misconceptions about Heaven is that it's quiet, still and somber with floating clouds and softly played harps. While all of this may be true, it is not the sum total of what Heaven is like. There are all kinds of noises, excitement and celebration in Heaven. "*And I heard something that sounded like a huge crowd, like rushing water and powerful thunder. They said, Hallelujah! The Lord our God, the Almighty, exercised his royal power! Let us rejoice and celebrate, and give him the glory, for the wedding day of the Lamb has come…*" (Revelation 19: 6-7)

"*I tell you that in the same way, there will be more joy in heaven over one sinner who repents than over ninety-nine righteous persons who need no repentance.*" (Luke 15:7)

HEAVEN HAS COMPLETE HEALING & RESTORATION

When we dig deeper into the characteristics of Heaven, we see it is the original framework of what earth is supposed to be. The book of Revelation shares with us one of the systems in place for healing and restoration SOURCED from God's river in Heaven. This is why disease, sickness nor pain exists there. Heaven has a continual flow of God's river with healing virtue running throughout the city by way of the Tree of Life. This is the same tree of life that was in the Garden of Eden. THE tree of life hydrates and brings perpetual wholeness.

"And he shewed me a pure river of water of life, clear as crystal, proceeding out of the throne of God and of the Lamb. In the midst of the street of it, and on either side of the river, was there the tree of life, which bare twelve manner of fruits, and yielded her fruit every month: and the ***leaves of the tree*** *were for the* ***healing of the nations***. (Revelation 22: 2).

HEAVEN HAS A GOVERNMENT

Heaven's government is the ultimate authority that rules over all things. When Jesus was sent to earth, He came to re-establish Heaven's government on earth. "For unto us a child is born, unto us a son is given: and the government shall be upon his shoulder: and his name shall be called Wonderful, Counselor, The mighty God, The everlasting Father, The Prince of Peace." (Isaiah 9:6) The Government of Heaven houses the Courts of Heaven, which governs all. (See Chapter 6).

The important thing to remember as we journey through this book is that we have been granted access to Heaven and its fullness. When Jesus died, the veil was torn; the partition between God and us was destroyed. What does this mean to us??? Glad you asked! It literally means GOD'S WORLD is made available to us ONCE AGAIN! We now have access to engage in Heaven and heavenly realms; access back to the FATHER! This access bridges the gap between Heaven and earth and produces an open Heaven where we can receive God's wisdom, God's direction, God's blueprint and strategies, and God's governmental authority. We can now engage Heaven and bring back what we need to establish God's Kingdom in the earth.

Let's look at some examples of Revelators/Ambassadors who went to Heaven and operated here in the earth.

1.) Jesus THE CHRIST

Jesus, The Christ, THE ULTIMATE Revelator and Ambassador of Heaven. He was the word and was there from the beginning. The word (Jesus) became flesh and was born in the earth. One of His missions was to bridge the gap between Heaven and earth. Thereby, reopening access for us to engage Heaven. As He ministered throughout the land, He constantly referred to himself as being one with the Father and manifesting the original intent of God's will for man. He was able to access Heaven and establish Heaven's Dominion in the earth.

"[19] *Then answered Jesus and said unto them, Verily, verily, I say unto you, The Son can do nothing of Himself, but what He seeth the Father do: for what things soever He doeth, these also doeth the Son likewise.*[20] *For the Father loveth the Son, and sheweth Him all things that Himself doeth: and He will shew Him greater works than these, that ye may marvel.*" (John 5:19)

2.) John the Revelator

John was the beloved Apostle of Jesus from the original 12 disciples. Rulers sought after John to persecute and kill him. When John was exiled and sent to the Isle of Patmos, he did not die as they wanted him to, but he was very much alive when he was caught up into Heaven. John was shown great mysteries in Heaven, which he brought back to earth.

Rev. 1: 4 "*John to the seven churches which are in Asia: Grace be unto you, and peace, from him which is, and which was, and which is to come; and from the seven Spirits which are before his throne;*"

Rev. 1: 10 *"I was in the Spirit on the Lord's day, and heard behind me a great voice, as of a trumpet,"*

Rev. 4: 1-2 *" After this I looked, and, behold, a door was opened in heaven: and the first voice which I heard was as it were of a trumpet talking with me; which said, Come up hither, and I will shew thee things which must be hereafter. And immediately I was in the spirit: and, behold, a throne was set in heaven, and one sat on the throne."* John referenced being IN THE SPIRIT a few times. For some, this may translate as an unction from the Holy Spirit or that he was only speaking in tongues. However, when John stated he was IN THE SPIRIT he was referring to literally being in Heavenly realms.

3.) Paul - The Apostle

The Apostle Paul was a very strong and influential apostle in the New Testament. He started out as a persecutor of the saints in the early church. Soon he was transformed to the point where even his name was changed from Saul to Paul. He was saved to spread the gospel of Christ to the utter parts of the world. After his conversion, He spent three years in the desert *(I believe that most of that time was spent praying in tongues and learning more of Jesus).* Paul was noted for sharing some of the revelations he received from Holy Spirit concerning our role as sons and ambassadors, in Heaven and in the earth.

"Even when we were dead in sins, hath quickened us together with Christ, (by grace ye are saved; And hath raised us up together, and made us sit together in heavenly places in Christ Jesus:" (Ephesians 2: 5-6)

Paul was one who was intensely focused on Heaven. He constantly admonished the church to focus on HEAVEN and not on the things or distractions of this world. *"If ye then be risen with Christ, seek those things which are above, where Christ sitteth on the right hand of God. Set your affection on things above, not on things on the earth."* (Colossians

3:2) Paul had many experiences going in and out of Heaven and the heavenly realms. He shared those experiences with us as much as he could in his letters to the churches in the New Testament. The revelations and blueprints he shared were weighty revelations, many of which we are still being equipped with in our lives today.

"[2] *I knew a man in Christ above fourteen years ago, (whether in the body, I cannot tell; or whether out of the body, I cannot tell: God knoweth;) such an one caught up to the third heaven.* [3] *And I knew such a man, (whether in the body, or out of the body, I cannot tell: God knoweth;)* [4] *How that he was caught up into paradise, and heard unspeakable words, which it is not lawful for a man to utter.*" (II Corinthians 12: 2-4)

Paul's access to Heaven allowed him to take entire territories and saturate them with the gospel of Christ. His access to Heaven also afforded him with what was known as his special brand of miracles. *"And God wrought special miracles by the hands of Paul:*
12 So that from his body were brought unto the sick handkerchiefs or aprons, and the diseases departed from them, and the evil spirits went out of them." (Acts 19: 11-12).

Paul carried major power and authority over the enemy. This type of access was not limited those in the New Testament. There were chosen Old Testament individuals who God gave special access to Heaven EVEN before Christ died on the cross.

4.) Ezekiel The Prophet

Although Ezekiel was a prophet from the Old Testament, he had access to Heaven and Heavenly realms. This access came through portals and openings that were afforded to him due to his prophetic mantle.

"[2] T*hen I beheld, and lo a likeness as the appearance of fire: from the appearance of his loins even downward, fire; and from his loins even upward, as the appearance of* *brightness, as the colour of amber. [3] And he put forth the form of an hand, and took me by a lock of mine head; and the spirit lifted me up between the earth and the heaven, and brought me in the visions of God to Jerusalem, to the door of the inner gate that looketh toward the north; where was the seat of the image of jealousy, which provoketh to jealousy.*" (Ezekiel 8: 2-3)

5.) Joshua The High Priest

Joshua was a High Priest in the Old Testament before Jesus was born. However, this depiction in Zechariah reveals how the High Priest position required supernatural access behind the veil. In this passage Joshua is standing before the Lord in a court room setting in Heaven with satan there to resist him (bringing accusation against him). However, the Lord rebuked satan and promised a Joshua authority in earthly and Heavenly. This would set Joshua up to be positioned to govern in the earth with access to Heavenly position and operations.

"*And He shewed me Joshua the high priest standing before the angel of the Lord, and satan standing at His right hand to resist him. 2 And the Lord said unto satan, The Lord rebuke thee, O satan; even the Lord that hath chosen Jerusalem rebuke thee: is not this a brand plucked out of the fire? 3 Now Joshua was clothed with filthy garments, and stood before the angel. 4 And he answered and spake unto those that stood before him, saying, Take away the filthy garments from him. And unto him he said, Behold, I have caused thine iniquity to pass from thee, and I will clothe thee with change of raiment.*
5 And I said, Let them set a fair mitre upon his head. So they set a fair mitre upon his head, and clothed him with garments. And the angel of the Lord stood by 6 And the angel of the Lord protested unto Joshua, saying, 7 Thus saith the Lord of hosts; If thou wilt walk in my ways, and if thou wilt keep my charge, then thou shalt also judge my house, and shalt also keep my courts, and I will give thee places to walk among these that stand by." (Zechariah 3: 1-7).

There are also Modern Day Ambassadors & Revelators who have experienced going to Heaven and are operating in bringing Heaven to the earth.

1.) Jessie Duplantis

Jessie Duplantis is currently a prominent pastor in New Orleans. Early in his ministerial career he had a visit from God that later led to his extraordinary visit to Heaven. He went to heaven, body, spirit and soul, and was there for about 6 hours. He testifies how he saw Abraham and David, to name a few. He was even able to see his own mansion that was waiting for him in Heaven. One of the most distinctive parts of his visit was when he experienced going to the throne room and seeing Jesus in preaching with fire and passion, encouraging those there that He was going to save their loved ones.

Years later when Hurricane Katrina came to destroy the city of New Orleans, Jessie used his God given authority and took dominion over his land, his church and his area. The hurricane did not damage his land at all. You can see his powerful testimony on YouTube or you can read more detail in his book, "Close Encounters of the God Kind".

Here's an excerpt from his book:

> "From my trip (to Heaven), I understood Heaven in a truly physical sense. It's a real place. I know that Heaven is a fact. It's beyond a hope; to me it's the reality. But people don't have to believe me, the proof of what I experienced is the fruit in the lives of the people who receive the message. People have asked me, "Why did the Lord take you to heaven?" I didn't know. He could have taken one of them, and He may still - I'm not a unique individual by any means. But then one day it dawned on me why He took me to Heaven…I'm willing to give Him anything I have, and I know He's willing to give me everything He has.[1]"

2.) Kat Kerr

Kat Kerr is a modern-day Revelator from Florida. Almost every single day God catches her spirit up to Heaven and reveals its world and the operations for her to share with those on earth. Kat has been going to Heaven for several years. She gives an eyewitness account of how saints (those who accept Christ) are transitioned from earth to Heaven after they die. She also witnessed some of the saint's loved ones residing there and living their most amazing lives in Heaven. Kat has addressed some contradictory myths about Heaven by sharing truths about Heaven's world. The fact that Heaven's culture is fun: its full of food, full of music, full of life, full of Godly entertainment and the Father's love. Kat has had countless interactions with the angelic realm and the Godhead. She has gathered armies of people to prepare them for Heaven's Invasion. She is constantly revealing the Father's plan and timeline for the incoming movement of Holy Spirit in the earth. You can read about her experiences in Heaven in her book Revealing Heaven Part I & Part II.

Here are some excerpts from Kat's book:

> "I would like to begin by explaining what God told me, that earth is a copy of Heaven. In other words, most of what is here on earth already exists in Heaven. It is not a flat place in the sky, floating around covered in clouds with fat baby angels dropping grapes into our mouths. IT IS A LITERAL 'WORLD'; round, just like earth, only huge in proportion. Hebrews 8:5 talks about things on earth being a shadow and type of what is in Heaven. Many things here (earth) have always been there (Heaven), only perfect! No death, decay, rust or pollution at all! Everything is beautiful - almost beyond description. God-inspired ideas eventually made it into the mind of man and were then invented here on earth. All 'good' things created came down from the Father (James 1:17). It is our enemy, satan, who is perverted and defiled things on this earth and he uses people to promote and defiled things on this

> earth and he uses people to promote and desire these wicked things neither evil nor its influence in Heaven…
>
> I have been caught up to Heaven, like John in the book of Revelations, for the purpose of sharing it with others…God has caught me up hundreds of times to Heaven and I am always awestruck by the beauty and life that exists there…As we enter into a Holy season of Heaven being poured out on this earth so we might do the greater works, you need to prepare yourself and your family to do more than just watch it come; you need to be ready to MAKE it happen! If you are serious about being a part of the Great Awakening (Joel 2) then you will surrender (everything) as I have. It will be everything, to gain Him (life itself)." [2]

3.) Shawn Bolz

Shawn Bolz is a modern day Revelatory who lives in California. He spent some of his foundational years at IHOP (International House of Prayer). He has been to Heaven and has seen the Body of Christ being trained and prepared as they were going in and out of Heaven to receive blueprints and execute them in the earth. He conveys messages from Heaven on a continual basis; to encourage the body of Christ and further the body in the direction of establishing Heaven in the earth. He often encounters the angelic realm and receives maps, plans, and strategies for Heaven's wealth and supernatural power to invade the earth. Shawn Bolz is also the founding pastor of Expression58 Christian Ministries and author of many books, namely *Growing up with God*. He has discovered strategies to train the youth in how to be open to Heaven and opened their access to God.

> "The devil resist and even prostitutes the subject of eternity for us, because Satan is jealous of our role in it. Keeping us from eternity is his ultimate goal. Satan works overtime to distract us from who we are and to occupy us in lesser roles. If he can

> do this to the Church, he will continue to dominate the world, because we have failed to engage in a rightful Kingdom dominion."[3]

4.) Justin Abraham

Justin Abraham is a modern-day Revelator and seer gift from the United Kingdom. He has experienced the Heavenly realms for years and has brought back revelatory instruction for the Body of Christ. There are several supernatural signs and wonders that accompany his ministry. Justin is constantly accessing Heaven realms, engaging with the Godhead and operating in the courts of Heaven. He's had many divine encounters with angels and Heavenly beings that have unveiled the mysteries of accessing Heaven.

Here are a few excerpts from his blog:

> "I've been consumed with a theme – it moves me everyday. The theme of experiencing and actually seeing that unseen dimension called Heaven. Yes I know Heaven is all around us in us, in Creation and People, and the Earth is precious and full of His glory but that's not what I'm talking about specifically here. I mean actually seeing, hearing and touching the invisible- being present in Heaven. This is the Mystic realm of God. Where like Paul we say "whether in the body I don't know- but I was hijacked into Paradise." It's what many of the Saints of old walked in and shared numerous stories of being swept into it."[4]

> "I believe engaging Heaven is ESSENTIAL- not only to understanding world events but also to shape world events. Paul believed engaging Heaven was NORMAL. Paul clearly said *"Seek those things above, set your mind on them, relocate yourself mentally"* (Col 3:1-2). Paul did not mock people for this Heavenly desire, but encouraged it as a KAINOS (new) lifestyle. He pointed us Heavenward (Phil 3:14) in Christ.

> Paul said in his Sacred Letters, that we are seated there (Eph 2.6) and have a function there now. We can wrestle there (Eph 6:12), are blessed there (Eph 1:3), and can learn from there (2 Cor 12:4) in ecstatic states of bliss. Paul taught we are Heavenly citizens with FREE ACCESS to the Throne of Grace (Heb 4:16) and Mount Zion (Heb 12:2). In fact Paul said this is where our true, real, higher life is now located hidden in Christ (Col 3:3). This is our new Reality. Jesus Himself encouraged this trans-dimensional thinking. Our dear Rabbi, said, "I am the Door! If anyone enters by Me, he will be saved, and will go IN and OUT and find pasture. (John 10:9). We have the ability to shift between dimensional worlds…Jesus, Heavenly Dimensions, Angelic Beings, Saints and Ever-Living people, Transportations and Remote Sight, Understanding the Courts and Government… a new normal is slowly emerging."[5]

5.) Ian Clayton

Ian Clayton is powerful modern-day Revelator and seer from the United Kingdom. Ian has spent over 32 years pressing into the presence and intimacy of God. He is continually accessing Heaven and the Courts of Heaven receiving game changing revelation from God and bringing it to the earth. He has received authority and backing from Heaven's Courts to stop earthquakes, save cities, transform molecular cells, and stop the hand of the enemy against entire countries. He has a major assignment to establish Heaven in the earth. His life is an example of the results of one who interacts with angels, Heavenly beings and most importantly the Godhead. Ian reveals major revelation about operating in the heavenly realms in his book, Realms of the Kingdom, Volume 1.

> "The reason we struggle with things of the spirit is because we have not understood this principle: God lives inside of us and we can touch Him on the inside of ourselves. What God wants is to be real to us, because He lives inside us we can embrace His presence inside us. Here is the most exciting thing when you

encounter the Kingdom of God that is within you. This Kingdom will transition you into the Kingdom of Heaven that is on the outside of you, without any struggle, because it is this Kingdom of God that transfers into the Kingdom of Heaven. It is this Kingdom inside that seats you in another position. No longer is there wrestling in the realm of the spirit in going to the realm of Heaven. No longer is there any struggle. Why? Because this Kingdom of God inside me takes me from here and puts me right over into the Kingdom of Heaven. When I am there I can enjoy it. I can enjoy what God does and I can enjoy the things of Heaven that are there. We have the capacity to do that, but it is a learned process. So we need to practice."[6]

6.) The Ladies of the Golden Candlestick

This was a group of about 20 ladies and a few men in the 1940's all attending the same Bible Institute in California. They some how ended up in the same place on their school's campus where they ALL received the same word from God. God challenged them to give up their pursuit for a public platform of preaching/teaching to seek only Him instead. In turn, God would bless them beyond measure with unusual signs and wonders. God also promised to raise up a powerful game changing minister from their area to help transform this world as a result of their continual intercession. After such instructions, they decided to gather 6 days a week, 8 hours each day to pray in the home of Frances Metcalfe (she was the leader and set person of the group). Before long, they were having frequent angelic visitations. Soon after, an actual door began appearing in Frances' basement where they were gathering, giving them access to Heaven. After so many years of accessing Heaven, being transported in the Spirit to other countries to minister, and conducting healing sessions, they finally encountered the young man whom God promised. This young man was birthed out of their commitment to fervent prayer and sacrifice. His name is Dr. James Maloney. He is currently a modern-day Revelator, who has experienced thousands of encounters in Heavenly realms. He has ministered thousands of miracles, signs and wonders alongside Jesus Himself. (We will discuss him later in the book). He honored this group by writing a 3-volume book that shares the story of their journey.

Excerpt written by Dr. James Maloney:

> “I don’t know of another ministry that was blessed with the same level of rapture and translation, similar to the experiences of Elijah and Philip. When I say that members (often several at a time) were transported, I mean physically - they disappeared and were taken to another part of the world for evangelistic campaigns, sometimes for several days at a time. In these instances they were supernaturally sustained, either by the people they met or through the angelic host. Often the Spirit would translate them to a country so that they might gain strategy on how to combat hindrances to the gospel, etc. They would then bring back these reports so the whole group could pray together. In this way, great moves of God were birthed throughout many nations. All of the earthly translations and rapture were separate from the translations to heaven, where many would return with sandals entwined with strange jewels, vest-like garments inset with twelve stones representing the tribes of Israel, headdresses arrayed in almost living colors, articles of clothing that would be stitched with gold thread - I mean the metal, not the color. These were the regular occurrences with the ladies of gold. It is not much of a stretch to say they were as often in Heaven as on earth...These kinds of transcendent encounters although they grew in deeper expression and manifestation as the following material shows, were constant and continuous for over fifty years, starting from day one when they gathered together.
>
> I recall seeing a door in the sanctuary, beautifully molded, emanating in a golden hue. I assumed when people walked though it, it led to another part of the house. Many years later, when walking through the house in the daytime with Marion Picard (Frances’ personal assistant, and the second-to-last original member alive beside Dora) I was stunned to realize the door was not there. It was explained to me

that door was a special door to Heaven. I didn't bother asking further details-they wouldn't have provided anyway." [7]

7.) Ana Mendez Ferrell

Ana Mendez Ferrell is a great modern-day Revelator that was converted from being a satanic priestess to a potent fivefold ministry gift. She was young when she experienced a visitation from Jesus. After that overwhelming time with the Lord she desired more but was deceived and influenced to join the satanic church. While in that demonic regime, satan visited her to take her as one of his brides but she refused. Once she refused he came after her relentlessly. She loss custody of her kids, and she could no longer work in her profession. The enemy tortured her so until she ended up in a mental hospital. One day a preacher came to that hospital, prayed for her and she received her deliverance. The very next day she was ministering under the power of the Holy Spirit with the diversity of tongues. She spent some foundational time with C. Peter Wagner's ministry. From that point she began operating in the realms of the supernatural. The Spiritual realm was opened to her and she continued in hundreds of signs, wonders, miracles and the raising of the dead. She has given life-changing revelation to the Body of Christ about the operation of the Heavenly realms, deliverance from the regions of captivity and freedom from the system of the spirit of Babylon, which carry the plots, and plans of the enemy. Ana and her ministry team traveled to Mt. Everest reclaiming that territory back to God. This was territory that had been 'claimed' by the witches and warlocks of that mountain. When Ana and her team went up to tack that territory back for the Kingdom of God, the mountain crumbled and yielded all the souls that were bound back to God. Ana and her ministry have literally been in the depths of the sea, reclaiming Heaven's Dominion in the waters and experiencing the sea yield itself back to God. She has pioneered the re-establishing of Heaven's Dominion in the earth's physical territory. The range of land and territory she has conquered ranges from mountains, valleys, oceans, frozen landscape, cities/regions and surrounding areas. These were all set free from the enemy's tyranny and brought into the Dominion of God. She reveals the keys of bloodline/DNA issues and bondages in her books; Iniquity, Regions of Captivity, and Seated in Heavenly Places.

Excerpt from Ana's book

> "I *began to have extraordinary experiences in the Spirit. I have been taken to Heaven many times to see and understand things that have been hidden for generations but that God wants to reveal to us. A new apostolic and prophetic generation is rising up all over the world, an ever-advancing army that cannot be stopped, a people of God who will move in the power of the greatest signs and wonders in history. The glory of Jehovah will truly be seen in them, and kings and the powerful men of the earth will run to them in order to be with Jesus. God is calling us to understand the deep things of His Kingdom, to enter into spiritual levels we never before dreamed of or imagined. God is calling us to change our earthly, human way of thinking with its limited levels of faith. He wants to convert us into real PEOPLE OF THE KINGDOM, sons of God who the devil cannot stop, or close doors to, a people with the dominion and authority of God to govern the earth Christ.*" [8]

This is not an exhaustive list of all the modern-day revelators and generals that exist today. However, I encourage you to take the time to search those that were and are Heaven's Ambassadors in the earth. Please know that as we greatly appreciate those that were and are operating as God's Ambassadors, God truly desires to use all of us as Ambassadors in one way or the other. That's why it's important to get a foundational understanding about the concept of Heaven's Dominion. It is a key factor in establishing the Government of God in Heaven and the earth.

THE COURTS OF HEAVEN

The Court System of Heaven is an integral part of the Government of Heaven. In fact, the Court System of Heaven is a literal and pivotal operation of God's Government. This system is not a metaphor, or a simile but it is an actual real, functioning place in Heaven where God's justice is administered on our behalf. Since earth is a shadow of Heaven so many of our systems originated in Heaven, particularly the governmental systems.

Although our court system in the United States is only a tiny shadow and example of Heaven's Court system, comparing the two will give us a frame work to build on. The three branches of Government in the United States are the Executive, Judicial, and the Legislative branches. Although the function of each branch in Heaven is greatly expanded, the same 3 branches of the United States Government can be found in the Government of Heaven as well.

- **Executive** - Our Sovereign God: In whom the supreme executive power is vested
- **Legislative** - functions in creating and establishing laws
- **Judicial** - interprets law and administers justice

As all of these branches impact our lives in one way or the other, in this section, we will focus on the judicial branch, more specifically its Court System. Within the Judicial branch of God's government is the Court system of Heaven.

Functioning in the courts of Heaven's judicial system does NOT mean you are using another model or template that shows you how to pray. I repeat, it is NOT JUST another 8-step way to pray. The Court system of Heaven is as REAL as the very breath you take each day. This system has made pivotal impact within the lives of mankind since the days of the bible. It is this system, the Government of Heaven that rules our lives, this universe, the galaxies and everything in between. If nothing else is grasped within this section of the book, please understand that Heaven is THE HIGHEST GOVERNMENT THAT DOES AND WILL EVER EXIST! Therefore the Court System of Heaven carries the Highest

Authority PERIOD!. The 'buck stops' there! God sits as the Highest Authority, Judge and King in Heaven. "*Let every soul be subject unto the higher powers. For there is no power but of God: the powers that be are ordained of God.*" (Romans 13:1) Not only is it THE HIGHEST GOVERNMENT, but also it will CONTINUE TO INCREASE! That's right, it will NEVER CEASE to INCREASE meaning his government will continue to supersede and exceed any form of legalities that exist!

"*Of the increase of his government and peace there shall be no end, upon the throne of David, and upon his kingdom, to order it, and to establish it with judgment and with justice from henceforth even forever. The zeal of the Lord of hosts will perform this.*" (Isaiah 9: 7)

This scripture in Isaiah confirms that Heaven's Government administers and establishes JUDGEMENT and JUSTICE FOREVER! God is waiting for us to start operating in His government as He designed us to from the beginning. Therefore, when we begin to engage with the government of Heaven AS SONS OF GOD, we have THE FULL BACKING OF HEAVEN in our lives because God, the Judge over all has supreme and final rule over EVERYTHING. When we get Heaven's FULL AUTHORITY, destinies, assignments and Dominion can be fulfilled. Justice can fully infiltrate every area of this world! This is a powerful revelation, and if we grow in it, we will begin to see insurmountable retribution for our lives and the lives of people across the globe!

The Courts of Heaven are literal places in Heaven where our governmental rulership as the church and Bride of Christ is executed. It is in this place that we receive a deeper level of authority and insight regarding how to execute God's will in the earth.

The word for Church in the Greek is the word (ekklēsia). This means the called-out ones, a governing body and assembly of the people convened at the public place of the council for the purpose of deliberating. **(12)** As one may be able to tell, the terminology used in this definition indicates that the word ekklēsia references a governmental body and/or a form of a court system. It's not a coincidence that God chose this word to define the church. One of our many roles as the church is to exercise our governmental authority in Heaven in addition to having or going to church. Our gathering as a body in church should teach us how to walk in the authority and Dominion required to operate in Heaven's system.

Therefore, this means that a part of the church's or the ekklēsia's assignment is to stand with Jesus in carrying out the responsibilities of God's Government and His judicial system. To handle this governmental responsibility, it's vital to understand more about its function and God's destiny for this earth. And guess what this points back to? That's right, it leads us directly back to Heaven's Dominion having full authority in the earth. The destiny of every person, every church, every city, every state, every country and every continent was designed to be a part of God's amazing plan to take back the world that HE created.

Therefore, when the enemy gets persistent about coming against God's plan for our lives, our churches and our territories, God has His judicial system in place. This system is designed to administer His justice against the wicked schemes of the enemy. The Court system of Heaven brings judgment to our enemies, and arrests satan's actions that fight against the destiny God has for us. This makes the path clear for HEAVEN'S HOST to transport the power of God FROM HEAVEN into the earthly realm. When the enemy is holding up our destinies, we can take those situations to the Courts of Heaven to get a verdict that will release what is being held up in our lives.

If there are any legalities or laws that have been broken and they are still on our record, the enemy can use these crimes or broken laws to bring accusations against us in the Courts of Heaven. If these accusations are not cleared, the enemy can stand on these legalities and ask for the judgment or punishment according to the law. God is a righteous judge and will stand by His word so He will have to judge according to His law. However, when the legalities (accusations) against us in the Court System are removed, we untie God's hands and He then has the legal right, according to His law, to grant judgment in our favor. This allows God to stop the enemies that are coming against us so that we can walk in the original intent of His destinies and promises for our lives. We can see an example of this in Daniel 7.

"*A river of fire poured out of the throne. Thousands upon thousands served him, tens of thousands attended him. The COURTROOM was called to order, and the books were opened. I watched as this horn was making war on God's holy people and getting the best of them. But then The Old One intervened and decided things in favor of the people of the High God. In the end, God's holy people took over the kingdom."* (Daniel 7: 10 & 21-22 MSG)

In this scripture you can see where the enemy held up and came against the saints to the point where he was prevailing. However, when the courts were seated, and the judgment of the Lord was rendered, the situation turned in the saint's favor. This is a powerful demonstration of God's government at work in our lives!

Let's discuss the Courts of Heaven a little bit more. As stated before, the Courts of Heaven and the courts in the earth have similar functions, positions and protocols. In fact, the overall purpose for both courts is fundamentally the same: to administer justice. However, when we refer to the Courts of Heaven, the purpose is exponentially expanded at least a billion times more! The enemy has weaved a very intricate web of injustice to stifle and stop the plan God designed for the earth. The enemy has strategically placed traps of principalities, wickedness in high places (Ephesians 6:12) to derail God's movement piece-by-piece, person-by-person, and territory-by-territory. Then he influences these areas of our lives and the areas of our world with darkness and confusion. The enemy's goal is to pervert and ultimately stop the will of God. Over the decades and generations, satan's influence has grown so strong to the point where it has caused a great rebellion against God. This rebellion has resulted in sickness, poverty, sexual and drug abuse, murders, rape, and even premature death. None of these are the will of God for our lives as His children. Sure trials, testing, and challenges come, but we were guaranteed an abundant life through Christ. *"The thief cometh not, but for to steal, and to kill, and to destroy: I am come that they might have life, and that they might have it more abundantly."* (John 10:10) This abundant life is to show forth the glory of the Kingdom of Heaven through us in the earth!

Operating in the Courts of Heaven gives us the highest platform to set things back into proper alignment and to re-establish God's Dominion in the earth through us. When the enemy comes against us with accusations in court, it causes our destiny and assignment to be stifled and stagnant. However, as God's children, we have the legal right to petition the Courts of Heaven and clear any accusations against us. "*Let us review the situation together, and you can present your case to prove your innocence*" (Isaiah 43: 26, NLT). When we bring a case before the Lord in court, we are joining the mediation team with Jesus by standing in the gap as legal representatives to bring God's justice. HE HEARS OUR CASES AND JUDGES THEM ACCORDING TO HIS WILL AND HIS WORD! This is one of THE greatest revelations ever!!!

When we stand in the gap and 'war' over our situation or contend over the will of God for our lives, the battle should BEGIN in the COURTS with the supernatural authority and backing of Heaven's Government. Robert Henderson is a powerful fivefold ministry gift and a modern-day pioneer of the revelation of the Courts of Heaven. He has written several books regarding the revelation God gave him about operating in the courts of Heaven. This is a portion of what he wrote regarding standing in the gap in the government of Heaven.

> "*Whether it is on a national level or a personal level, the devil does not want what is in the books to come into reality on the earth. This is why there were such extreme attempts by satanic powers to keep Jesus out of the earth. Remember that the devil tried to exterminate the Jewish race several times. This was to remove from the planet the race of people through which Jesus would be born. Then after He was*

born, Herod sent out a decree to kill all the babies within Jesus' age range. This was to try to destroy Him. Why was this done and many other things done? What was the purpose? It was to keep the Word from being made flesh (John1:14). It was to keep what was written about Jesus in the books of Heaven from entering the earth. This is true for anything that is written in Heaven. Whether it is nations, churches, businesses, individuals or any other thing, there will be attempts to keep what is in the books from coming into the earth realm. Satan does not want the word made flesh on any level. Everything that is written in the books about you, nations, kingdom purposes and God's desires will be contested.

The devil does not want what is written in the books to be born into the earth and be made flesh. It is our job to see this accomplished. A primary thing I want us to realize is that the conflict for what is in the books is in a courtroom and not on a battlefield. That is why when the court is seated in Daniel 7 the books are then opened. We are not on a battlefield. We are in a courtroom to get God's kingdom purposes into the earth. I know I have already said this, but I must continue to emphasize it because we must make this shift in our thinking. The protocol and manner of operation in a courtroom is different from that on a battlefield. We are seeking to get legal things in place for ultimate victory.

Another very important thing we must know about contending for books to come into the earth realm is that there are varying levels of courts in Heaven. Zechariah 3:7 shows us that the Lord promised Joshua, the High Priest, that if he walked in holiness, he would have a place to walk in the courts of Heaven." [9]

In the Old Testament, the High Priest would stand in the gap for the children of Israel's' lives and destiny. Once a year the High Priest would take the blood of lambs and goats, the red heifer, and other animals to clear the legalities (sins, iniquities, transgressions) of the people for that year. This was a legal transaction of mediating and standing in the gap between God and the people so that there would be no penalty of judgment against the people for the sins they committed that year. This was known as appropriating the sacrificed blood to cover all of their legalities for that year.

Now the greatest event that changed this process FOREVER was Jesus shedding his blood and dying for us as THE LAST AND ULTIMATE sacrifice for ANY AND ALL legalities. It was and still is perfect in every way.

> *"[4] For it is not possible that the blood of bulls and of goats should take away sins...[12] But this man, after he had offered one sacrifice for sins forever, sat down on the right hand of God;[18] Now where remission of these is, there is no more offering for sin. [19] Having therefore, brethren, boldness to enter into the holiest by the blood of Jesus, [20] By a new and living way, which he hath consecrated for us, through the veil, that is to say, his flesh;" (Hebrews 10: 4,12,18-20).*

So why do we still need to go to the Courts of Heaven when Jesus said, "It is finished" (John 19:30) and completed the finished works of the cross? So glad you asked! The redemptive story of man has many layers but can be simplified as this: When Jesus died, the price and the sacrifice needed to remove all sin was completed. The blood is for every ailment that mankind has or will suffer and it was shed to set everyone free from all bondage and captivity. The key here is that the blood must be appropriated. The High Priest took the sacrificed blood that was shed for the sins of the people and THEN appropriated it as instructed so that blood was applied for the purpose of clearing the sin.

> *"But if we walk in the light, as he is in the light, we have fellowship one with another, and the blood of Jesus Christ his Son cleanseth us from all sin.*
> *If we say that we have no sin, we deceive ourselves, and the truth is not in us. If we confess our sins, he is faithful and just to forgive us our sins, and*

to cleanse us from all unrighteousness." (I John 1: 7-9)

When Jesus died, he gave the last blood sacrifice needed to finish the SACRIFICE portion of the atonement process. Praise God!!! All of the sacrifice that was needed to clear the legalities of mankind was accomplished on the cross. HOWEVER, the APPROPRIATION portion of the atonement process is still left up to us. When Jesus ascended back to Heaven, He left the major role of the appropriation for the church. This is what the High Priests did in the Old Testament when they applied the blood of the animals on the altar to clear the sins of the people.

"*For the life of the flesh is in the blood: and I have given it to you upon the altar to MAKE an atonement for your souls: for it is the blood that maketh an atonement for the soul.*" (Leviticus 17: 11)

However, the church is now tasked to apply the blood of Jesus in every area of our lives. When we have sinned or when we have fallen short, we have access to the blood of Jesus so that we can apply it for the atonement of our sins so that it removes any other legality charged against us. "*And He is the propitiation for our sins: and not for ours only, but also for the sins of the whole world."* (I John 2:2)

The Courts of Heaven is one of the main places where, we appropriate the blood. The blood of Jesus is always THE KEY evidence that testifies on our behalf and clears any and all accusations of the enemy. Then the verdict can be rendered in our favor. Jesus was the lamb slain, so that we could be restored as a royal priesthood, to stand in the gap and appropriate His shed blood. Through mediation and operating in the courts of Heaven we can bring all things back into God's original alignment of peace, hope, abundance, and Heaven's dominance in the earth.

As you read further in this book, each chapter will provide more and more details about the courts of Heaven and the base we need to operate in God's Government. So, fasten your seat belts because there is so much more to come!

---

[1] Duplantis, Jesse. Jesse Duplantis Ministries: http://www.jdm.org
[2] Kerr, Kat, http://www.katkerr.com
[3] Bolz, Shawn. Bolz Ministries, https://bolzministries.com
[4] Abraham, Justin. "Time to Participate with Heaven, https://companyofburninghearts.wordpress.com/2013/04/15/blog-time-to-participate-with-heaven/
[5] Abraham, Justin. "Heavenly Encounter" https://companyofburninghearts.wordpress.com/2017/07/20/blog-heavenly-encounter/
[6] Clayton, Ian. Son of Thunder, https://www.sonofthunder.org
[7] Maloney, James. Dove on the Rise International Ministries
[8] Mendez-Ferell, Ana. http://voiceofthelight.com/main/
[9] Henderson, Robert. *Operating in the Courts of Heaven*

CHAPTER 2 REVIEW QUESTIONS

1. What is God's relationship to Heaven and Earth?
2. With the content that has been presented so far, please explain your depiction of Matthew 6:10.
3. Please give at least three aspects of Heaven with scripture reference.
4. Please explain how we are now able to access Heaven.
5. Please write about at least 2 biblical ambassadors that operated in Heaven and in the earth. Please explain how they accomplished this using scriptural references.

Chapter 3: Holy Spirit: The Key to Our Supernatural Life, The Base for operating in Heaven's Government

As we learned in the first chapter, God gave man the authority to have Dominion in the earth. If the assignment of Dominion is going to be successfully accomplished, man will need to learn how to engage with the most potent power source there is and ever will be…HOLY SPIRIT!

Most of the saints in the Body of Christ will agree that any task, especially one as monumental as establishing dominion, will need the power of God's Spirit to complete it. However, the part not so readily embraced is the operation of the gifts of Holy Spirit through which we engage the power of God. This is the power that raised Jesus from the dead. This is this same power that raises us up from our spiritual death; strengthening our spirits to rule and govern with Him. So, let's review some foundational truths about the Holy Spirit's role in the Godhead. This framework will put us on the same page as we take a more in-depth look into Holy Spirit's operation in the Government of Heaven.

The Nature of God

First, let's review three unchanging characteristics of the Godhead. This will give us just a tiny picture of who God truly is. It is imperative to understand these truths about God because they establish the immutability of His rulership in the Universe.

He is omnipresent: "Present in all places at all times."[1]

Holy Spirit is everywhere at the same time. "*Whither shall I go from thy spirit? Or whither shall I flee from thy presence? [8]If I ascend up into Heaven, thou art there: if I make my bed in hell, behold, thou art there. [9]If I take the wings of the morning, and dwell in the uttermost*

[1] https://www.merriam-webster.com/dictionary/omnipresent

parts of the sea; [10]*Even there shall thy hand lead me, and thy right hand shall hold me,"* (Psalm 139: 7-10).

A.W. Tozer, a very powerful Christian author said this,

"God dwells in His creation and is everywhere indivisibly present in all His works. He is transcendent above all His works even while He is immanent within them."

God's presence can be in Ohio, in Iowa, in Russia and in Africa at the same time. He has no boundaries.

He is omniscient: "Having infinite awareness, understanding and insight; having unlimited knowledge**."**

He knows EVERYTHING. There is nothing overlooked or hidden from God because He knows all things. "*Nothing in all creation is hidden from God. Everything is naked and exposed before His eyes,...*" (Hebrews 4:13 NLT)

Psalm 147:5 states this: "*Great is our Lord, and of great power: His understanding is infinite". God not only knows all things that have happened in the past in every part of His vast domains,* and He is not only thoroughly acquainted with everything that is now transpiring throughout the entire universe, but He is also perfectly cognizant of every event, from the least to the greatest, that ever will happen in the ages to come. God's knowledge of the future is as complete as is His knowledge of the past and the present. Even more than that, the future depends entirely upon Him.

A.W. Pink says it best: "Were it in anywise possible for something to occur apart from either the direct agency or permission of God, then that something would be independent of Him, and He would at once cease to be Supreme."

He is omnipotent: God is not only all-powerful, but HE is the one who created power. There is no power greater than the power of God! He is THE source of ALL power and gives us authority to use HIS delegated power in the earth. Revelation 19:6 tells us,

"...*Alleluia: for the Lord God omnipotent reigneth.*" He can live inside of all of us at the same time - at FULL capacity.

When we combine these three vivid definitions, it is still only a grain of mustard seed view of who the Godhead is to us. God is THE MOST WONDERFUL God, the ONLY God who CREATED ALL POWER, WHO HAS ALL POWER and is everywhere at the same time.

"*Now unto the King eternal, immortal, invisible, the only wise God, be honour and glory for ever and ever. Amen,*" (I Timothy 1: 17).

The Godhead

Let's go a bit further in our study of God. In the Godhead there is Father, Son and Holy Spirit. We are NOT referring to 3 separate Gods. We are referring to the ONE TRUE AND LIVING GOD. After He created the earth, He said "...*Let us make man in OUR image, after OUR likeness:..*" (Gen. 1:26). This tells us that the full manifestation of the Godhead created one of His most precious treasures, which is mankind. God said "Let us make man in our image," He reveals to us that He used all of who He is (Father, Son, Spirit) to create man to look and be like Him. Man is made as one being with one Body, Soul, and Spirit, which is the likeness of God.

Our spirit reflects the LIKEness of the Father's Spirit:

John 4:24: "*God is a Spirit: and they that worship him must worship him in spirit and in truth.*"

Proverbs 20:27: "*The spirit of man is the candle of the Lord, searching all the inward parts of the belly.*"

Ecclesiastes 12:7: "*Then shall the dust return to the earth as it was: and the spirit shall return unto God who gave it.*"

Our body reflects the LIKEness of Jesus, God in bodily form:

John:1 & 14: "[1] *In the beginning was the Word, and the Word was with God, and the Word was God...*[14] *And the Word was made flesh, and dwelt among us, (and we beheld his glory, the glory as of the only begotten of the Father,) full of grace and truth.*"

Colossians 2:9: "*For in him dwelleth all the fulness of the Godhead bodily.*"

Our soul reflects the LIKENESS of Holy Spirit.

Understanding how man's spirit and body are made in the likeness of Father and Son is straight forward and to the point. However when it comes to seeing how our souls are made in the likeness of Holy Spirit, this truth seems to be a little more nestled in the scriptures. Let's connect the dots by looking more closely in the scriptures.

The Greek word "Pnuema" is a term that is connected to the operation of Holy Sprit. This word means "a current of air, a vigorous breath; of Holy Spirit, representing the soul as the vital principle of life. This very concept is found in the book of Acts as the term 'wind' which describes the Holy Spirit's breath when He descended to earth. Acts 2 says, "*And suddenly there came a sound from heaven as of a rushing mighty wind...they were all filled with the Holy Ghost, and began to speak with other tongues, as the Spirit gave them utterance.*" (Acts 2:4)

This very same concept of the 'breath' of Holy Spirit was actually first seen in Genesis during the creation of man. It is taken from the Hebrew word 'n'shaman' which means "vital breath, divine inspirations [birthing] the soul.

When God created man in Genesis, He [The Godhead] "*...formed man of the dust of the ground, and* ***breathed*** *into his nostrils the* ***breath*** *of life; and man became a* ***living soul***," (Genesis 2: 7). Both 'n'shaman' and 'pnuema' come to life in this text, showing the handy work of Holy Spirit's divine breath birthing the soul of man.

It is with HIS power and HIS guidance that we partner with God to build an edifice, or a superstructure, inside of our spirit man to house the power of God. "*For we are labourers together with God: ye are God's husbandry, ye are God's building,*" (I Corinthians 3:9). Can you believe that AMAZING miracle? It's still hard for me to wrap my mind around the fact that my body houses the Spirit of the Lord! That truth alone could take up two volumes of books and we would still only be scratching the surface of what that truly means. WHAT an honor and privilege to have God Almighty living inside of us! For now we will stop right there and SELAH.

SATANS DEVICES

AGREEMENT
[THE OCCULT]

FEAR

TRAUMA

SIN

5SENSES

passions

feelings

emotions

GATES

THE SOUL

LAYERS

HOLY SPIRIT
SHOW ME THE ROOT!

DO NOT BE IGNORANT
OF SATAN'S DEVICES

BE YE TRANSFORMED
BY THE RENEWING OF YOUR MIND

PROSPER
AS YOUR SOUL
PROSPERS

GOAL: TO KEEP YOU FROM ADVANCING & FULFILLING YOUR SCROLL

Who is Holy Spirit?

"So, who is Holy Spirit *really*?", you ask? He is GOD! He is the ultimate, final authority who is over all the heavens and the earth! "*Thus saith the Lord the King of Israel, and his redeemer the Lord of hosts; I am the first, and I am the last; and beside me there is no God,*" (Isaiah 44:6). There is no other God anywhere.

When Holy Spirit comes to dwell inside of us, He brings His power with Him for us to utilize in the earth and in our lives. "*But ye shall receive power, after that the Holy Ghost is come upon you: and ye shall be witnesses unto me both in Jerusalem, and in all Judaea, and in Samaria, and unto the uttermost part of the earth,*" (Acts 1:8).

Holy Spirit is God, full of love, wonder and might. Because of this we worship Him, love Him, obey Him, and follow His leading. He knows ALL things and He, as the triune God, is the creator of all things good and perfect. He is beyond our laws of time, our laws of space and even energy. He is omnipotent, omnipresent, and omniscient along with Jesus and the Father and equally worthy of ALL our worship and adoration!

THE GIFT THAT KEEPS ON GIVING

It is imperative that we realize it is GOD HIMSELF who comes to live inside of us. One of the foundational things Holy Spirit does when He comes to live inside a redeemed believer in Christ is begin the process of transformation. Why do we need to be transformed? Transformation is needed so we can show the world God and His perfect will through our lives.

Romans 12:2 says, "*And be not conformed to this world: but be ye transformed by the renewing of your mind, that ye may prove what is that good, and acceptable, and perfect, will of God.*"

Holy Spirit brings the power to completely change our old DNA, which carries the sin nature passed down through the corrupt bloodline of Adam after he fell in disobedience. When transformation by Holy Spirit takes place, He enforces the finished work of Jesus at the cross and changes us into mature sons of God. "*Beloved, now are we the sons of God, and it doth not yet appear what we shall be: but we know that, when he shall appear, we shall be like him; for we shall see him as he is*," (I John 3:2). When we commit to this path of transformation, it brings us into mature sonship. This is when God can fully trust us with Kingdom responsibility. A major part of this responsibility is learning to operate in His Government, which is also a part of our inheritance as children of God. Operating in God's government requires the power of Holy Spirit.

So when we receive the baptism of Holy Spirit or the indwelling of Holy Spirit, we actually receive the GIFT AND THE POWER OF GOD! Peter preached this to the people present on the day of Pentecost. He said, "…Repent, and be baptized every one of you in the name of Jesus Christ for the remission of sins, and ye shall receive the GIFT of the Holy Ghost," (Acts 2:38).

Not only is Holy Spirit THE absolute BEST gift we could ever receive, but when Holy Spirit comes into our lives to dwell, He also comes with other gifts, administrations and operations. Let's take a look at 1 Corinthians 12.

"Now there are diversities of gifts, but the same Spirit. 5 And there are differences of administrations, but the same Lord. 6 And there are diversities of operations, but it is the same God which worketh all in all. 7 But the manifestation of the Spirit is given to every man to profit withal. 8 For to one is given by the Spirit the word of wisdom; to another the word of knowledge by the same Spirit; 9 To another faith by the same Spirit; to another the gifts of healing by the same Spirit; 10 To another the working of miracles; to another prophecy; to another discerning of spirits; to another divers kinds of tongues; to another the interpretation of tongues:" (I Corinthians 12: 4-12)

From this passage we can see that Holy Spirit IS THE GIFT THAT KEEPS ON GIVING! These gifts and operations of Holy Spirit actually are the many tools that aid us in our transformation.

One of these amazing gifts is often overlooked and misunderstood. This is the gift of divers kinds of tongues (also known as diversities of tongues). There are other types of tongues within this one gift, that we may not all have in totality. However, we all can receive the foundational gift of tongues for personal edification when we receive the baptism of Holy Spirit. This diversity is what some of the church mother's would refer to as 'your prayer language' or 'your Heavenly language'. This is the diversity of tongues that Jude referred to when he admonished us to build ourselves up praying in the Spirit. (Jude 20)

We see an example of diversities of tongues on the Day of Pentecost in Acts. Acts 2 says, "A*nd there appeared unto them cloven tongues like as of fire, and it sat upon each of them.* **4***And they were all filled with the Holy Ghost, and began to speak with other tongues, as the Spirit gave them utterance.*" (Acts 2:3-4) There is a key word in this verse that I would always glaze over. It is the word 'cloven'. This word cloven indicates, separation, divided into parts or sections. This definition establishes the fact that there were different types of tongues given when Holy Spirit came on the day of Pentecost. The different sections or DIVERSITIES of tongues that came on that day still come today when we are baptized in the Holy Ghost; especially tongues for personal edification.

When we are utilizing the diversity of tongues for personal edification, we are not talking to or with anyone but GOD! "*For he that speaketh in an unknown tongue speaketh not unto men, but unto God, for no man understandeth him, however it may be that in the spirit he speaketh mysteries,*" (I Corinthians 14:2). It is a heavenly language where God can talk to us Spirit to spirit, yet at the same time we are also talking to Him. Therefore, because it is an unknown language directly from God to our spirit, and from our spirit to God, not even the enemy can understand it.

When we utilize this gift of tongues for personal edification (also referred to as an unknown tongue) we are actually engaging in a conversation with Holy Spirit. It is a very intense, expedient conversation. It opens up our spirit to receive AND to give utterance to the mysteries He has written about our lives. Once the mysteries are downloaded into our spirit, we then begin speaking these mysteries out loud into the atmosphere through this unknown language. Therefore, some consider this to be the 'Perfect' prayer.

In this process, Holy Spirit uses our God ordained authority that was breathed into us when we became a living soul in the earth. Because God gave us dominion as earthen vessels, we have the authority to speak into the atmosphere to declare the will of the Lord in our lives AND in the earth. The destiny He created for us was written in each of our life's book as a mystery before we were even formed in our mother's womb. God told the prophet Jeremiah "*Before I formed thee in the belly I knew thee; and before thou camest forth out of the womb I sanctified thee, and I ordained thee a prophet unto the nations,*" (Jeremiah 1:5). Just like Jeremiah, God predestined us for a great work. As we pray in our Heavenly language, these mysteries are revealed and uttered into our spirit and into the earth's atmosphere.

So let's connect the dots about our prayer language. When we pray in tongues, mysteries go in our spirit AND mysteries come out of our spirit. These mysteries are given by the Spirit of God. Both of these things happen simultaneously as Holy Spirit gives us utterance to pray in unknown tongues and empowers us to do so. Isn't that cool!?!? This is a mystery in itself. A supernatural transaction that takes place as we pray in tongues!

"With that prayer language, He gets involved directly with you in a one-on-one relationship that is independent of anyone else, even of your own mind. When the Holy Spirit prays for you, He takes the plan He hears the Father utter and pours it through your spirit. And the language He uses to express that plan as it flows through you is the supernatural language of tongues. Every time you give the Holy Spirit opportunity, He will use that language to pray for your calling, to pray out the plan of God, to edify you, and to charge you with His holy power. He will lend Himself to you as your faith allows Him to be activated within your spirit." – Dave Roberson

Because satan can NOT understand the spiritual transaction of praying in tongues, he is not privy to what is being said. This causes him to be confused about what strategies he can use against us. Don't get me wrong; he does have devices set up against us that lie in waiting. The enemy has already gathered some information from our bloodlines, family patterns and even some things he may have heard us say. However, praying in the Holy Ghost (praying in tongues) puts up a shield around us to keep us from deception. The revelation we receive through tongues for personal edification also gives us wisdom about how to avoid the pitfalls and traps of the enemy. Therefore, through this supernatural transaction, we receive strength to resist satan. His tactics against us are thwarted. James 4 admonishes us saying, "*Submit yourselves therefore to God. Resist the devil, and he will flee from you.*" (James 4:7) The enemy has a much more difficult time blocking the aspects of our destiny from coming to pass because we have now prayed them into manifestation without him knowing what has actually took place. This type of prayer also builds a hedge around us to keep us protected from the enemy's deception. That is my kind of prayer!

So when we pray in tongues, we are praying in faith that Holy Spirit will lead and guide us into ALL truth about our lives, about who He is, and about the operations of the Kingdom of God. Scripture says, "*Howbeit when He, the Spirit of truth, is come, He will guide you into all truth: for He shall not speak of Himself; but whatsoever He shall hear, that shall He speak: and He will shew you things to come,*" (John 16: 13). We are trusting that Holy Spirit is going to pray through us as we yield our vessel to pray out what is needed the most. He is going to prioritize what should be prayed about when we speak in tongues because He knows all about our lives more than we do.

For example, we may pray in tongues seeking for God to give us a down payment on a house we are trying to buy. But we may also be avoiding the lying issue that needs to be rooted out of our lives. Because Holy Spirit knows there is a lying issue that needs to be addressed first, the words that are uttered in our Heavenly language as we pray are going to be about plucking up the root of that lying spirit that's holding up our transformation process. When we engage in this diversity of praying in tongues for personal edification, we don't dictate WHAT is being prayed. Holy Spirit is going to prioritize the prayer to address what's needed the most at that time in our lives. The Holy Spirit ensures that the completion of our transformation process can continue. However, what we can dictate or choose is when we pray, how often we pray and how long we pray in tongues! This is so cool.

When I was a teen, I used to think a special move of God in the church service had to come over me in order to start praying in tongues. I've since learned that I can pray in tongues for personal edification whenever I want, to as long as I want to. When I began to realize this truth, I was elated!

It was then that I began to discover that the revelation, truth, wisdom, peace and healing that accompanied this life of praying in the Spirit. We can edify our spirit man everyday by deciding to pray without waiting for an emotion or a special anointing to come over us. Once we begin praying in the Spirit, the edification process that leads to full transformation begins immediately! If I want to engage in our Heavenly language one hour a day or 4 hours a day I can, and it will intensely increase the strength of my spirit man![2]

As we pointed out in the Book of Acts, there are other diversities of tongues demonstrated on the day of Pentecost. When you keep reading throughout Acts chapter 2, you will see that every tongue under Heaven was represented and each man hearing them identified with the tongues the disciples were speaking. Let's look at that scripture:

> *"And they were all filled with the Holy Ghost, and began to speak with other tongues, as the Spirit gave them utterance.* ***5*** *And there were dwelling at Jerusalem Jews, devout men, out of every nation under heaven.* ***6*** *Now when this was noised abroad, the multitude came together, and were confounded,*

---

[2] *Walk of the Spirit, Walk of Power: The Vital Role of Praying in Tongues*, Dave Roberson, pg.

because that every man heard them speak in his own language," (Acts 2: 4-6).

This is the diversity of tongues that is a sign for the unbeliever. This is when Holy Spirit ignites this gift of speaking in a known language on the earth so that an unbeliever can hear the words of the Lord and be saved.

However, the diversity of tongues that is for personal edification is the type of prayer to which Jude refers. "*But ye, beloved, building up yourselves on your most holy faith, praying in the Holy Ghost,*" (Jude 20). This a language that God has also created for our individual edification process. This specific diversity of tongues that provides personal edification[3] affects our total person. It addresses every area of our lives to ensure that we are truly being transformed.

PRAYING IN TONGUES: A MAJOR KEY

As we just discussed, when we pray in tongues we also give Holy Spirit permission to pray through us the mysteries of God. He then uses the authority that was breathed into us at man's creation to utter these mysteries in the earth. He is praying through us mysteries that were established in the Heavens from the beginning.

"But WE SPEAK THE WISDOM OF GOD IN A MYSTERY, even THE HIDDEN WISDOM, which God ordained before the world unto our glory: Which none of the princes of this world knew: for had they known it, they would not have crucified the Lord of glory...But GOD HATH REVEALED THEM UNTO US BY HIS SPIRIT," (I Corinthians 2:8).

Operating in God's Government requires the guidance, knowledge and understanding of Holy Spirit. In order for us to know how HE operates, our base of operating in the Spirit must be fortified to handle the level of responsibility and revelation needed to carry out this task of rulership and Dominion.

---

[3] *Walk of the Spirit, Walk of Power: The Vital Role of Praying in Tongues*, Dave Roberson, pg. 48

So let's take a closer look at what I Corinthians 2:8 is referring to when it speaks of mysteries. Simply put, a mystery is anything that you do not know. This can range from not knowing how angels are created to not knowing why you act the way you do. Yes, that's right. A mystery is defined as this "something not understood or beyond understanding." We know there are millions of mysteries regarding God, His Kingdom and the realms of Heaven. Holy spirit reveals ALL things to us; all mysteries pertaining to God and to our lives. He reveals them in the order and manner we need to receive them, no matter how big or how small. As we pray in the Spirit, He gives us downloads of revelation and information that is needed to fulfill our destiny. What an amazing God He is!

One of the gentlest and most unassuming modern day revelators I've ever met was also one of the most powerful men I've ever encountered. His name is Dave Roberson from Tulsa, Oklahoma. Years ago in the late 70's and early 80's, God sanctioned Dave to write a book about the LIFE CHANGING revelation he received regarding praying in tongues. This book is called *The Walk of the Spirit, the Walk of Power: The Vital Role of Praying in Tongues.* This is one of the passages from his book.

> *"The very measure of God's power in a believer's life is dependent on how much of his life is ordered by the Holy Ghost…Step by step, He has taught me how to walkout of a life dominated by the flesh into a new life dominated by the Holy Spirit through the matchless gift of praying in my heavenly prayer language."*[4] – Dave Roberson

When Dave gave his life to the Lord, he began to get hungry, and even desperate, to live in the real, tangible presence and power of God. Like some of us, he searched and searched, wondering what was the key to operating in the Spirit realm with power and manifestation. He began to study people like John G. Lake, Smith Wigglesworth and Kenneth Haggin. Anytime a preacher or prophet would come into his town, after a powerful worship service he would ask them questions like, "How did you hear God like that?" and "How were you able to move and operate in miracles and in the prophetic ministry like

---

[4] *Walk of the Spirit, Walk of Power: The Vital Role of Praying in Tongues*, Dave Roberson, pg. 5

that?" To his disappointment, the answers were vague or ambiguous and left him in the same predicament; many questions with no answers.

Early in his life, he felt the Lord called him into full time ministry. In his search for understanding the anointing and how other men and women of God were able to operate in the Spirit, his results fell short of any tangible answers. So Roberson decided to pray 8 hours a day as he prepared for the ministry opportunities to come. He pointed out that he did not hear God specifically tell him to pray 8 hours. He felt that if ministry was his full time job then he should put in the work of praying which would be the equivalent of a full work day. (He recounts his story in his book in Chapter 2). His first week of prayer he would run out of things to pray in English only after about 15 - 30 minutes. So he felt to just begin to pray in tongues continuously.

During the next weeks and months of praying in tongues, he would only take a lunch break then go back into prayer. He did not necessarily get the goose bumps of the anointing every time he prayed. In fact, in one of his teachings he described the actual praying in tongues to be as dry as "cracker juice". However, something inside of him was still determined to keep going. Then, one day after a few months of praying in tongues 8 hours a day, Dave received an invitation to visit a church in the neighborhood and he went. While the preacher was preaching, Roberson began to see that there was something wrong with the leg of the person sitting beside him. He described it as if he was seeing an X-Ray in the spirit realm. He leaned over to the lady and asked if she wanted her leg to be healed, and she said yes! So he began to pray for her leg and it was healed. Of course, this stirred up a lot of commotion. Roberson was asked to come back that night to minister by some of the ladies of the church.

When he returned to the service that night, he was told he had to minister in the basement. When he arrived in the basement there was a crowd waiting for him. The elders of the church were present, not wanting him to minister. But before they could get to him, Roberson stood up on the stage and called for anyone who wanted the Holy Ghost to come forward. Before he knew it, he was laying hands on people and person-after-person began to receive the infilling of the Holy Ghost with the evidence of speaking in tongues. Many people were being delivered and set free that same day!

He ran out of the meeting crying asking God what just happened. God responded,

> *"This anointing didn't come on you because of your calling, your creed, your color, or your nation. It came upon you because you have uncovered a spiritual law: praying in other tongues for your personal edification. That law carries with it an ironclad guarantee to build you up on your most holy faith in your spirit — that part of you from which faith comes. You have found something you can do on purpose to edify yourself — as much as you want to, as long as you want to, whenever you want to."*[5]

The Spirit of the Lord told Roberson that he had discovered a major key about the law of praying in tongues. After building a life of walking in the Spirit by way of praying in tongues and the other spiritual disciplines (prayer, fasting, the word, etc.), he went on to do many healings, miracles, signs, wonders, and receive major revelations as many of God's generals did throughout history.

The concept of walking in the Spirit is found in Galatians 5 where it says, "Walk in the Spirit, and ye shall not fulfill the lust of the flesh," (Galatians 5:16). I found it interesting that in the English standard version of this text states, "But I say, walk by the Spirit, and you will not gratify the desires of the flesh." In the Living Translation version of this scripture it says"...I advise you to obey only the Holy Spirit's instructions." And the New living translation version of the scripture it says, "So I say, let the Holy Spirit guide your lives." In multiple versions of this text it points out how a life IN the Spirit is how you combat the flesh. It's not just something you do when there is a crisis, but it is a walk that we are to engage in everyday. This is how walking in the Spirit becomes our lifestyle.

---

[5] *Walk of the Spirit, Walk of Power: The Vital Role of Praying in Tongues*, Dave Roberson, pg. 25

Edification through praying in tongues

So, you may be asking, "What is edification and why do we need it?" I'm glad you asked that question! The main root word of edification is the word 'edifice' which is a Latin based word. Merriam-Webster breaks down the definition like this:

> *"In Latin, the noun tense of the word is "aedes", which means "house" or "temple,". This is the* ***root*** *of aedificare."*[6]

The root word in verb tense is 'edify' which means "to erect a house." In other words, to edify is to build a house or temple.

Putting these concepts together in the context of our study, we can define the term "edification process" as follows: *The edification process is the process by which God builds a spiritual superstructure in order for us to house the anointing, the power and the operations of God.*

Inside every redeemed person who has joined the body of Christ through salvation in Jesus, there is a spiritual superstructure that needs to be strengthened and established so that Holy Spirit can live and operate inside of it. One of the major keys to a successful edification process is, praying in tongues.

When we pray in tongues for personal edification, we are literally building a spiritual edifice within our spirit man. This gives us the necessary strength and wisdom to house the anointing power of God. We cannot do what we need to do in our lives and HIS Kingdom if we are not edified and built for the task. More importantly, we cannot be completely transformed into the image of Christ and become who we are destined to be as sons of God if we do not undergo the edification process.

As we go through different levels of the edification process, our minds are renewed and our inner man becomes strengthened. This allows us to carry more and more of the operation of the Spirit in our lives. However, submitting to this edification process can be

---

[6] Merriam-Webster Dictionary, https://www.merriam-webster.com/dictionary/edify

difficult because of how strong the sin nature is and how our flesh just refuses to die. In fact, it seems like the very MOMENT many give their lives to the Lord, trouble, challenges, tears and struggles increase. The internal war becomes painfully real. This is because of the way the edification process transforms us. Transformation begins to take place inside of our spirits and souls, directly killing the flesh (our sinful nature) inherited when Adam and Eve sinned. The tension that is felt during this process is the flesh fighting to stay alive.

Let's park here for a minute and highlight some of Pauls writings about his struggle during his edification process:

"[21]I have discovered this principle of life—that when I want to do what is right, I inevitably do what is wrong. [22] I love God's law with all my heart. [23] But there is another power[e] within me that is at war with my mind. This power makes me a slave to the sin that is still within me. [24] Oh, what a miserable person I am! Who will free me from this life that is dominated by sin and death? [25] Thank God! The answer is in Jesus Christ our Lord. So you see how it is: In my mind I really want to obey God's law, but because of my sinful nature I am a slave to sin," (Romans 7:21-25).

When Paul wrote this passage in Romans, some time had passed since his initial, drastic conversion on the road to Damascus. Therefore, when he wrote these passages, Paul had been saved, filled with the Spirit and walking in power. He ministered to many different churches and was revered as a notable apostle in the Lord's church. Yet Paul was candid about the tangible struggle taking place between his spirit man versus the carnal man (also known as our flesh). The carnal nature was first awakened in mankind when Adam and Eve ate of the tree of the knowledge of good and evil. Adam received direct instructions from God NOT to eat of that tree, but they did. This disobedience marked his DNA with a corrupted nature that was passed down to us. This is the carnal nature that dominates our lives before we receive Christ and begin our journey toward transformation.

The carnal nature is so strong that even though Paul had a desire to obey God, he admitted the struggle to fulfill this desire was very real due to the pull of his carnal nature.

However, Paul knew how gravely important it was to continue his edification process in the Spirit because in the next chapter this is what he says. *"For to be carnally minded is death; but to be spiritually minded is life and peace."* (Romans 8:6)

Romans 8:7-8 goes on to tells us " *Because the carnal mind is enmity against God: for it is not subject to the law of God, neither indeed can be.* [8] *So then they that are in the flesh cannot please God.*" Our bodies are the temple of the Holy Spirit. This temple also houses our spirit man and our spirit man contains the superstructure to which I have been referring. This spiritual superstructure needs a very strong foundation laid by God Himself.

> *"For we are labourers together with God: ye are God's husbandry, ye are God's building.* [10] *According to the grace of God which is given unto me, as a wise masterbuilder, I have laid the foundation, and another buildeth thereon. But let every man take heed how he buildeth thereupon," (I Corinthians 3: 9-10).*

This supernatural structure or house within us is designed to carry the revelation and resonant power of God. Therefore, the edification, or building up, of our spiritual edifice speaks to a long term structure inside us that has longevity and carries the strength, and potency of the Spirit.

It is easy to settle for the pseudo-wisdom and strategies of the world to build ourselves into good citizens. However, the strategies of this world will not be able to give you the wisdom needed to build an eternal structure fit for the Kingdom.

I Corinthians 3 says it well: "*Let no man deceive himself. If any man among you seemeth to be wise in this world, let him become a fool, that he may be wise.19 For the wisdom of this world is foolishness with God. For it is written, He taketh the wise in their own craftiness..*" (I Corinthians 3: 18-19) Something as lasting and potent as legacy and inheritance takes God's wisdom to build, and it takes time to produce fruit that remains. This is why edification is so important. It is not a process that can be skipped over. The flesh does not fight fair and does not die easily. The flesh will do everything to keep you from being transformed because it does not want to die. However, if we stick with the process and deliberately live a life of killing the flesh & edifying our spirit man, we will experience the abundant full life Jesus came to give us.

Paul became transparent in the scriptures sharing his weaknesses and the painful peril of his journey during his edification process. Paul's edification process was not just receiving Jesus as his Savior. It was also about allowing Christ to become his Lord. Many of us are aware that it's one thing for Jesus to save us from the destination of hell, but it's a whole other process for Him to become our Lord. When He becomes our Lord, He is the final authority in our lives. He is the one we obey and to whom we surrender knowing all He has us do is for our good. The flesh HATES this because that means the death of the carnal man.

Placing his flesh under subjection to Christ in obedience to Him is what Paul learned to do. The key factor in that last phrase is that Paul *learned* to place his flesh under subjection to Christ. Paul's elevation to walking in power and authority was not an overnight, 'one and done', 'quick fix' type process. Paul yielded himself to be transformed by the edification process in his walk in the Spirit. Paul began to walk in so much power and authority that God allowed him to perform a special class of miracles.

> *"[11] And God wrought special miracles by the hands of Paul: [12] So that from his body were brought unto the sick handkerchiefs or aprons, and the diseases departed from them, and the evil spirits went out of them," (Acts 19: 11-12).*

Paul's submission to God brought about his walk of power; and this walk was rooted in his edification process. Paul gave us a great example of what a Christian's submission to the Lord and walk in the Spirit should look like and can be.

When Paul first received salvation, he actually went into the dessert for about 3 years searching, praying for and receiving many, many revelations about Christ; who He is and who we are *in* Him. He gave himself over to the process to walk toward a lifestyle of transformation, revelation and deliverance through prayer, especially through praying in tongues. At one point in I Corinthians, He even states this: "I thank my God, I speak in tongues more than ye all..." (I Cor. 14:18). This is the same man who is attributed to writing more of the New Testament than any one person. I honestly believe the large amount of time Paul would spend praying in tongues is one of the main reasons why he received such life changing revelations. Paul submitted to the edification process and received massive revelation knowledge pertaining to Kingdom mysteries. This is one of the major benefits that come from praying in tongues.

Living a life IN Christ is vitally necessary if we are to become fully matured sons of God. This means we should choose the plan He laid out for our lives and submit to the edification process to fulfill that plan. It does not mean becoming a robot; not in the least. We are not slaves, but we are His sons and we have the freedom to be who we were originally designed to be. However, living life in Christ does mean we must live our lives His way, according to His plan and His will. He is our creator and he created us to show how beautiful and wonderful He is through us. When we establish a lifestyle of praying in tongues, it not only begins the edification process that 'untethers' (disconnects) us from the world's system, it also joins us to the technologies of Heaven.

Through the gifts and administrations of the Spirit, The Holy Ghost pours into us and ignites inside of us the methods and blueprints of Heaven. This also includes the administration and wisdom we need in order to sit in the seat of Heavenly Government we were created to occupy.

Spiritual Disciplines: Practical tools for a Supernatural Life

Engaging in the spiritual discipline is one of the most potent ways for us to receive the downloads and strategies concerning this path of governing in Heaven. Along with praying in tongues, the other disciplines also edify us unto fulfilling God's will for our lives. Holy Spirit partners with us in this process to aid in building a supernatural infrastructure and base of operation within our spirit man. This process allows revelation to flood our lives about God's world and about His design for us to rule and reign with Him. If we are going to take this journey of attaining governmental authority in the Kingdom of God, building a solid foundation in Christ is not an option. Yet at the same time, it is one of the most wonderful privileges one could ever have. "*But there's far more to life for us. We're citizens of high heaven!...*" (Philippians 3:2 MSG).

The edification process is a process that we have to continually engage in until the day we are completely transformed. Praying in tongues is a part of what we do to build ourselves up, allowing Holy Spirit to complete the supernatural part of the process. Engaging in the edification process is a part of building our walk in the Spirit. Therefore, it's not just Holy Spirit working but it is also us partnering with Him. A basic list of the spiritual disciplines include praying, fasting, studying scripture, consecration and worship. Let's look at the analogy of physical exercise is a good comparison to applying the spiritual disciplines. If you exercise for 2 minutes once a week or even 10 minutes once a week, it does very little. I can't say it does nothing, but it doesn't give you much of the benefits that could be gained, including, good circulation, stable blood pressure and weight management to name a few. You see only a very small amount of these benefits, if any with just that amount of exercise. However, if you were to exercise 1 hour a day, in about a week or two you will begin to experience marked positive changes in your blood pressure levels, cholesterol and your general health. This is similar to how praying in tongues works. The more you pray in tongues, the more benefit you will begin to see in your entire life. We are not talking about the 30 seconds of praying in tongues some of us may do during church every now and then. We are referring to intentionally spending a solid amount of time praying in tongues everyday. The more you pray in tongues, the more it impacts our lives.

Dave Roberson says it this way:

> "With that prayer language, He gets involved directly with you in a one-on-one relationship that is independent of anyone else, even of your own mind. When the Holy Spirit prays for you, He takes the plan He hears the Father utter and pours it

through your spirit. And the language He uses to express that plan as it flows through you is the supernatural language of tongues.

Every time you give the Holy Spirit opportunity, He will use that language to pray for your calling, to pray out the plan of God, to edify you, and to charge you with His holy power. He will lend Himself to you as your faith allows Him to be activated within your spirit. He will pull you out of everything Jesus set you free from and into everything Jesus says that you are in Him.

If you want to, you can go into your room and pray in that supernatural language for two, four, or even twelve hours, and God the Holy Spirit will create every single word that comes out of your mouth. It is your choice to pray or not to pray. But every time you do choose to pray, you will come out of that time of prayer more edified in His plan and purpose for you than if you hadn't done it."[7]

When we take care of our physical bodies, we basically address this by doing the right exercises, eating the right foods, drinking the right amount of water and getting proper rest. Just like with our physical man, there are different tools or methods we use to build, maintain and better the spiritual superstructure within our spirit man.

There are certain tools and methods throughout the Bible that have been shown to help strengthen our walk in the Spirit and enable us to achieve tangible success in our edification process. As unpopular as the spiritual disciplines seem to be in 2018, they are proven, practical tools that yield great and lasting results. If used correctly, they will establish strength, potency, maturity, and longevity in our relationship with God. This is the very base we need in order for us to operate in the Government of Heaven. The five items below are the basics of what we call the 'spiritual disciplines'.

1. Prayer
2. Scriptures (Study)

---

[7] *Walk of the Spirit, Walk of Power: The Vital Importance of Praying in Tongues*, Dave Roberson, pg. 8

3. Fasting
4. Consecration
5. Worship & Intimacy

This list includes just some of the basic spiritual disciplines that aid us in our edification process. There are so MANY benefits that come with each spiritual discipline that we do not have time to cover them all. If this is your first time applying all of these to your life, I challenge you to start engaging in these disciplines TODAY! If you are already applying any or all of these disciplines, I dare you to go deeper and don't just stop at 30 minutes or an hour. Extend your time and study. Whether you are new in the Lord or a seasoned warrior, here is the Spiritual Discipline Challenge we are daring you to take:

THE SPIRITUAL DISCIPLINE CHALLENGE

Here is the challenge: Take 4 Weeks and apply ALL of the disciplines. Then make sure you observe and journal the impact on your life as you get closer to God!

PLEASE NOTE:

The regiment of these disciplines are given to help get the best out of each tool that God affords us to have. It is not with a 'religious' or 'pharisaic' spirit that we recommend these tools. These recommendations come from our experience with seeking a real relationship with God. These are some of the main rudiments that we've seen set Godly patterns in our lives and in the lives of other believers. However if anyone is following any of these regiments out of habit or from a place of 'religion', ironically, these tools are still what will help you get out of that place. So I encourage to keep going either way. These tools will make notable impact in your life if applied on a consistent basis.

Suggested book about the spiritual disciplines:

This book was mentioned earlier in this chapter. This is one of THE BEST practical yet revelatory books I've ever read about the spiritual disciplines. It is a 'must read'. "The Walk of the Spirit, the Walk of Power: The Vital Role of Praying in Tongues." by Dave Roberson.

DISCIPLINE 1: PRAYER

Prayer builds our supernatural edifice to house potent power. It also builds our Godly relationships.

I'm sure by now we all get the point that prayer, especially praying in the Spirit is a NECESSARY, pivotal key to our walk in God. However, just in case you still need a little more proof, Ephesians 6 tells us this: "*Praying always with all prayer and supplication in the Spirit, and watching thereunto with all perseverance and supplication for all saints*;" (Ephesians 6:18). The Apostle Paul refers to this spiritual discipline of praying as a part of putting on the whole armor of God mentioned earlier in Ephesians 6. This is one of our major keys to withstanding the strategy of the enemy. It is also a very major step to building our relationship with God and becoming one with Him. A daily life of communication and intercession is vital in today's world.

Dr. Bill Hamon states it plainly:

> *"The Baptism of Holy Spirit was the main truth that was taught in the Pentecostal Movement in the first decade of the 1900s and the Charismatic Movement in the 1960s. I have focused more on pioneering and preaching the Prophetic- Apostolic Movement, which began in the 1980s; the Saints Movement, which is now underway; and the Third and Final Church Reformation. Now it has become apparent that revelation about the gift of the believer's spirit language needs to again become PRIORITY in the body of Christ."*

PRAYER CHALLENGE:

For 4 weeks, pray in tongues for 30 minutes every day. Then for 5-10 minutes make declarations and decrees over your life.

DISCIPLINE 2: SCRIPTURES

Scriptures transform our thought process. They prepare us to govern & walk in the power of God's word.

The scriptures of the Bible house the word of God. It is so important to learn the heart of what God is saying to us and the history of how He operates through daily scripture reading. The word of God allows the mind of God to be within us so that we can think His thoughts and have His wisdom and perspective concerning His Kingdom. This is very key so that we know how to govern according to His will and His ways. With His word, we make decrees and declarations over our lives, knowing that His Word does NOT return to Him void.

"So shall my word be that goeth forth out of my mouth: it shall not return unto me void, but it shall accomplish that which I please, and it shall prosper in the thing whereto I sent it." (Isaiah 55:11).

SCRIPTURE CHALLENGE:

1. For 4 weeks, research and study a specific passage of scripture. Choose one chapter per week. They can all be from the same book of the Bible or from various books based on a singular topic like love, justice or prophecy. This is not to study for a sermon or lesson, but to apply what you learn to your life and your relationship with God.

2. For 4 weeks, along with the prayer challenge, find and meditate on scriptures relating peace, prosperity, healing and sonship and declare these scriptures over your life daily. .

DISCIPLINE 3: FASTING

Fasting kills the flesh, unbelief and fear. It addresses the hidden issues in our lives.

This is one of the spiritual disciplines that people hate the most. I admit, I am in that number (written with a smile). However, it is so important to fast from food and beverages on a regular basis, such as once a week. It is key to incorporate a few periodic, extensive fasts throughout the year as well. When the disciples could not cure a certain boy in the scriptures who was said to be a lunatic, Jesus told them that is was because of their unbelief. He went further to say that this type of unbelief can only come out by prayer AND fasting.

> *"Then came the disciples to Jesus apart, and said, Why could not we cast him out? 20 And Jesus said unto them, Because of your unbelief: for verily I say unto you, If ye have faith as a grain of mustard seed, ye shall say unto this mountain, Remove hence to yonder place; and it shall remove; and nothing shall be impossible unto you. 21 Howbeit this kind goeth not out but by prayer and fasting," (Matthew 17: 19-21).*

When we fast, we are directly killing the flesh and addressing the hidden doubt that is in our lives. When fasting is coupled with prayer, it is a dynamic force against our flesh, fortifying our spirit man.

Suggested book about fasting: "The Way of the Eagle" by John Arcovio

FASTING CHALLENGE:

Within a 4 week period, along with the prayer and scripture challenge, fast at least one day a week from food and beverage with the following schedule.

Day 1- Week 1: Fast from 12 midnight to 4:00 p.m.

Day 2 - Week 2: Fast from 12 midnight to 6:00 p.m.

Day 3 - Week 3: Only 1 meal in a 24 hour period

Day 4 - Week 4: Fast 24 hours

DISCIPLINE 4: CONSECRATION

Consecration sets us apart, draws us closer to God. It guards us from the demonic external influences.

Some often interchange this discipline with fasting but there is a marked difference. When Jesus was referring to fasting in the Bible, he was specifically referring to abstaining from food and beverages as we stated above. However, consecration is referring to separating ourselves from the world and taking deliberate actions to get closer to God in our hearts, our thoughts and in our everyday actions. For example, this would include abstaining from excessive social media, television and secular music. When consecrating, we take deliberate action to cut out any of these type of distractions for our lives and purposely set aside time to spend with the Lord. Consecrating 'untethers' us or disconnects us from the spirit of the world and binds us to the Spirit of God.

The Levitical Priesthood was set apart specifically for the business of God's worship in the Old Testament. Since Christ came, all who are believers are now His chosen priesthood. We are called to live a life set apart for His Glory. "But ye are a chosen generation, a royal priesthood, an holy nation, a peculiar people; that ye should shew forth the praises of him who hath called you out of darkness into his marvelous light;" (I Peter 2:9). We could write another separate book on this subject alone, but to sum it up, 'we are what we eat'. So if we digest the things of the world, we take on its spirit.

1 John 2 tells us "Don't love the world's ways. Don't love the world's goods. Love of the world squeezes out love for the Father. Practically everything that goes on in the world—wanting your own way, wanting everything for yourself, wanting to appear important—has nothing to do with the Father. It just isolates you from Him. The world and all its wanting, wanting, wanting is on the way out—but whoever does what God wants is set for eternity," (I John 2:15 MSG). This is why consecrating and tearing away from carnal things to engage in Heavenly things is vital for the renewing of the mind and building a life close to God.

CONSECRATION CHALLENGE:

Within a 4 week period, eliminate all secular music, all secular television and reduce your social media interaction.

Week 1 - Monday - Friday: No secular music/television; limited social media.

Week 2 - Monday - Friday: No secular music/television; limited social media.

Week 3 - Monday - Friday: No secular music/television; limited social media.

Week 4 - Monday - Friday: No secular music/television; limited social media.

DISCIPLINE 5: WORSHIP & INTIMACY

Worship and intimacy open us to God's supernatural love exchange. They cause oneness & closeness with God.

Living the life of a worshipper actually has to do with submitting to Him as Lord in whatever He has designed for us to do. "But the hour cometh, and now is, when the true worshippers shall worship the Father in spirit and in truth: for the Father seeketh such to worship Him," (John 4:23). Out of this lifestyle comes an expression of intimate worship and praise. This is what we are referring to with the discipline of worship and intimacy.

Our mysterious yet beautiful connection to God in worship is one of the most amazing experiences we could ever have. Being raptured in the waves of His presence while in the midst of intimately worshipping Him is unforgettable. It is easy to get lost in the strength of His gentleness where just a touch of His love resonates throughout your entire being.

> *"...He is a mighty savior. He will take delight in you with gladness. With his love, he will calm all your fears. He will rejoice over you with joyful songs," (Zephaniah 3:17).*

Connecting with God in intimate worship on a daily basis is a priceless privilege. It binds our hearts with Him like no other way can. Worship is a major key to becoming one with Him. It is in the true intimacy of worship where a type of surgery in our hearts takes place.

This transaction exchanges our version of love for God's. I dare you to get lost in His presence and see Him through the eyes of Truth & Love.

WORSHIP AND INTIMACY CHALLENGE:

Within a 4-week period, spend at least 30 minutes worshipping and praising God. Along with extolling Him, and expressing His worth and loving kindness to you, spend time loving Him in your heart. Take those moments to be grateful for what He has done and think solely on His attributes and His love for you. Express this through music, singing, poetry, letters and through giving Him verbal expressions of your love for Him and what He means to you.

Example of the Spiritual Disciplines Challenge (Combined)

So, if we put all the challenges together, one day in your challenge week would look something like this:

MONDAY:

- Praying in tongues - 30 minutes
- Worship & Intimacy - 30 minutes
- Scriptures - 30 minutes
- Present your petition/Decree over your life - 10 minutes
- Fast: 12 midnight to 4:00 p.m.

Consecration: No secular music/television; limited social media

Yes, this challenge will probably require for you to get up early in the morning and/or even stay up late at night. It is a sacrifice; that's why they are called 'the disciplines". However once this becomes a regular part of your life, you will wonder how you even lived before. Then, you will notice that you will begin to long for more time with God.

This is when you should start to have fun with the challenge and get creative with Holy Spirit. Draw, paint, write, sing, express your love to Him in multiple ways! Pour out your heart to God and let him pour back into you! Let it become the time that you look forward to; seeking HIM and all of who He is in your life!

He is waiting for you in this place of intimacy and is even more excited about the time you are going to spend with Him than you are! As you get closer to HIM, you will be able to live a life in His world like you've never imagined. It will be your oneness with Him that will lay the foundation you need to live supernaturally and to operate in His Kingdom as He originally intended. So get ready to open your heart and go a little deeper in God. Become one with His heart and let Him become one with yours.

CHAPTER 3 REVIEW QUESTIONS

1. In whose image are we created? Please explain of what three main aspects man is composed?
2. What is one of Holy Spirit's foundational objectives when He comes to live inside of us?
3. What is the edification process?
4. What role does playing in tongues play with the edification process?
5. Please list what this chapter refers to as the "Spiritual Disciplines". Please briefly give a definition of each one and how they help build your spirit man.

SECTION I: DOMINION QUIZ

1.) Dominion is... (Please pick only one answer)

a. Control
b. Politics
c. Authority & Governance
d. Kings, Queens, Presidents, Sovereigns

2.) Please explain the concept of Godly Dominion in the earth.

____

____

____

3.) Please explain why man getting exiled from the Garden of Eden was so detrimental.

____

____

____

4.) a. Define Enmity.

____

____

____

b. What event addressed enmity? How?

____

____

____

5.) Name 5 aspects or characteristics of Heaven.

____

____

____

6.) The following were ALL considered Revelators/Ambassadors in the scriptures.
(Please pick only one answer)

a. Aaron, Judah, and Simeon
b. Adam, David, and Paul
c. Ruth, Moses Joseph-Mary's Husband
d. Leah, Jesus, Sarah

7.) Please pick at least one modern day Revelator/Ambassador and explain why they are 'labeled' a Revelator/Ambassador.

____
____
____

8.) What are the Courts of Heaven?

____
____
____

9.) Please explain the difference between the sacrifice of the blood versus the appropriation of the blood.

____
____
____

10.) Please explain the role of the Body of Christ as it pertains to operating in the Courts of Heaven.

____
____
____

11. How were we made in the image of God? (Please pick only one answer)

a. Mind, conscience, intelligence
b. Breath, water, earth
c. Life, love and happiness
d. Body, spirit, soul

12. Please explain the edification process.

____
____
____

13. a. What are one of the main tools we can purposely use throughout our edification process?

____

____

____

b. Please explain how this tool aids in this process?

____

____

____

SECTION II: CO-LABORERS

Chapter 4: Being Co-laborers with Christ

The phrase "co-laborer with Christ" was foreign to me until my college years. Even after that introduction I never really understood what it meant. A church I was attending while in college gave me my first introduction to the concept of "the Kingdom of God." It was here I learned about man's authority and responsibility as stewards of God's Kingdom in the earth. It was a truly revelatory experience for me.

I learned that God placed authority to transform my life and make a difference in this world squarely in my hands. It is my privilege and responsibility to "do business until He comes," as the parable in Luke 19 states. Let's dissect this parable further. This parable speaks of a great nobleman who leaves his home to go receive a kingdom. He leaves his servants to do business and multiply his holdings while he is gone. The scripture referenced the nobleman leaving his servants mina, a form of currency. A mina unit represented a substantial amount of money. One mina equaled about 100 drachmas. One mina was also worth about one quarter of an agricultural worker's annual wages.[x] Multiply the mina by 10 and in one day you would've earned a person's earnings for two and half years.

Could you imagine your boss entrusting you with his business with such a great amount of wealth to continue operations while he or she went on a long trip? You would be responsible for every aspect of the business. This was exactly what happened in this parable. The nobleman's expectation was for his servants to implement what they were taught to increase the value of the estate while he was away. For those who acted wisely, they were given cities to rule in the nobleman's new kingdom. Why? Because they understood the value of being a co-labor with their master. I am certain they had no idea the reward or inheritance their obedience would bring.

But what about the one who didn't "do business" until the nobleman returned? What was his inheritance? Well, what he had was taken away because he did not accomplish the will of his master and did what seemed right in his own eyes. However, what seemed right to him was not pleasing to the one he served and not in keeping with how he managed his domain.

This parable was a sobering moment for me. I usually approached such parables with this mindset, "Well, I better figure out how to live right and do something great... I don't want God to be disappointed with me and take away the little I have." Such a pessimistic outlook, right? This was not the right outlook because I did not have the relationship with God to understand what these parables meant.

Firstly, we must understand the importance of developing an intimate relationship of friendship and love with God; and that we are chosen to co-labor with Him. I lacked this same understanding early in my journey with God. Then, one day the revelation suddenly hit me: I was created to work with Him! Until that moment, this parable was just another vague story. I came to the realization it was the key to fulfilling my dominion mandate in the earth and an invitation to greatness. Why is co-laboring necessary? It's a necessary component in establishing the Kingdom of God on earth. How so? Our faithfulness must be proven! We must be faithful to grow what we already know, then God will bring the increase. The lessons learned from the small moments in our lives build character for what's ahead. As we engage with those around us in our everyday lives, our families, friends and co-workers, we are being prepared for greater things. Therefore, we must be mindful to steward those relationships and places of influences well.

For instance, learning how to settle an argument with my best friend will in turn teach me how to better mediate conflict at work. The same skills of mediation and conflict resolution are essential to being a business owner as well. If I master these methods of communication, I can then negotiate partnerships and business ventures well and be an asset to other companies. By mastering the art of communication with those close to me in my season of preparation, I learn an invaluable relationship skill that will be very helpful in the broader scope of my life. In reviewing this example, we can see that I am allowing God to develop me. As I allow this work of processing if you will, God can in turn increase my mina, or the scope of my authority and responsibility, in His Kingdom!

Next, it is imperative that we see ourselves with the right perspective, and through the right lens. The right perspective assists us with understanding the "how" of what we are called to do. The slave with one mina lacked confidence in himself to meet his master's expectations. Which begs the question; why did he still receive one mina? It's my belief that the nobleman knew the slave had the potential to do something with it. As previously explained, one mina was a very valuable portion or investment.

The slave with one mina chose to bury his portion. This act is direct reflection of the slave's perspective on the investment he received from his master. By burying his portion, he: 1) lacked the master's vision for his estate. 2) inadvertently discounted, or devalued, what was given to him. How many times have we done the same with God and His kingdom? We are a part of God's kingdom and must serve His agenda. By serving His agenda we say "yes" to experiencing true success in this life and know what it means to be great in God's kingdom.

Many of us operate as "the one mina slave." We've taken the most valuable, precious thing God has given us, and HID it! Our equivalent of "hiding the mina" is rejecting God's direction and will for us. We hide our mina, because we've discounted who we are in God. In our rejection of the Father and His plan, we ultimately reject ourselves. We badger our minds with those discounted thoughts and feelings: "I am too messed up to do anything great". "I only cause problems wherever I go, I don't want to hurt anyone, so I won't try". "I've never written a book before and I didn't even finish school. I won't be any good at it, so I won't even try." "I'm not good enough for her, how could I ask her to marry me? She deserves better." The thoughts of self-rejection affect our ability to see ourselves as heirs and co-laborers with Christ.

So, before we can begin to labor with Him, our perspective must change and come to a higher place of truth (the art of repentance)! The truth is, we are sons of God and co-heirs with Christ. It's from that place of knowing our identities where the real work can begin.

SONS OF GOD

To fulfill our mandate, of taking dominion over the earth and subduing it, we need the right perspective. We must understand who God is in us, who we are in Him and what we are called to do and why! As a child of God, we are not in this alone. In fact, we were never meant to build His kingdom apart from Him. However, we must do our portion! Someone may carry out our plans, but they lack our voice and unique imprint. God is many things to us, and one of the fundamental ways we relate to Him, is as our Father. Our Father has a vast domain. He created a Kingdom and then created man to rule over it. This earthly life is intended to groom and prepare us for dominion over creation. Imagine, this entire world was created by our Father to share with us! As I matured in my walk with God, I began to understand my role as a co-laborer with God was an honor. Once I gained God's perspective, being his co-laborer was no longer a chore or a burden.

Romans 8:12-17 tells us, *"[12] So then, brethren, we are under obligation, not to the flesh, to live according to the flesh— [13] for if you are living according to the flesh, you must die; but if by the Spirit you are putting to death the deeds of the body, you will live. [14] For all who are being led by the Spirit of God, these are sons of God. [15] For you have not received a spirit of slavery leading to fear again, but you have received a spirit of adoption as sons by which we cry out, "Abba! Father!" [16] The Spirit Himself testifies with our spirit that we are children of God, [17] and if children, heirs also, heirs of God and fellow heirs with Christ, if indeed we suffer with Him so that we may also be glorified with Him."* (NASB)

The question remains: Are we willing live by the Spirit and follow the amazing destiny God has predestined for our lives? Or will we live by the flesh and be governed by our fears, whims, bondages and the like? The answer: We will live by the Spirit, of course! The Holy Spirit was given as an earnest guarantee of our full redemption. What does that mean exactly? Holy Spirit guarantees the full manifestation and establishment of who we are, as Sons of God. According to Romans 8 we are fellow heirs in Christ. As fellow heirs with Him we identify with His suffering and the bearing of His burden for His namesake. Understand that the bearing of Jesus burdens qualifies us to experience and carry His glory.

Our suffering with Him brings our heart and mind into alignment with God. We begin to perceive life from His perspective in the suffering, if we allow Him to speak to us and mold us. As He begins to mold us our hearts become broken over the injustices and unnecessary pain others experience. We become outraged at the perversion of the gospel, we desire to see people experience God in a whole new way, and we are eager to build His kingdom His way. This is the true heart of a co-laborer at work.

BUT WHAT IS A CO-LABORER ANYWAY?

Before we go any further, I should probably define who or what is a co-laborer. The one requirement to be considered a co-laborer, is accepting Jesus as Savior and becoming a part of the body of Christ. To operate in the function of a co-laborer, the one redeemed by Christ must accept and operate in his position and responsibility as a child of God establishing His kingdom on earth.

As co-laborers, we work with God to fulfill His mission for the world. As such, the prefix co is critical to understand. "Co" implies there is a common goal of two or more individuals working together to accomplish that goal. In co-laboring with the Father His burdens become our burdens and He will not allow His standards to be comprised. In this form of partnership, each person has a role. When we look at the roles of co-laboring in the kingdom, its defined as children who are heirs of the divine kingdom of God. Yes, we are the Bride of Christ, a kingdom of priests, prophets, evangelists, teachers and more. However, the only way to become a child of God is to be birthed into the kingdom through our belief in Jesus.

John 1:12 says, *"But as many as received Him, to them He gave the right to become children of God, even to those who believe in His name,* [13] *who were born, not of blood nor of the will of the flesh nor of the will of man, but of God." (AMP)*

Let's explore what it means to be children of God the foundational construct of who we are in God's kingdom.

ASPECTS OF THE KINGDOM OF GOD

Being a co-laborer with God means we bear the burdens of Jesus, but again, not on our own. Jesus admonishes us to take His yoke upon us and learn of Him in Matthew 11:29. From this scripture, we know that we must strive toward humility and follow His lead. What does this look like in our daily lives? It looks like us intentionally taking on God's character, nature and cause. The establishment of the Kingdom of God on the earth is a great cause. Before we go any further let's look at what a kingdom entails.

Webster[xi] defines kingdom as:

1. a politically organized community or major territorial unit having a monarchical form of government headed by a king or queen
2. the eternal kingship of God
3. the realm in which God's will is fulfilled
4. a realm or region in which something is dominant

I love these definitions! The kingdom of God is a realm in which God is dominant and He reigns as the supreme monarch. He governs and determines all aspects of its operation including the political system. If we take this one step further: Let's, consider what makes a kingdom a kingdom?

I've taken the liberty to comprise a list; it's not exhaustive, but comprehensive.
A kingdom requires: a mission, a mandate, a monarch, other rulers to help administrate the work of running the kingdom, finances, buildings, education, arts and entertainment, judicial systems, governing systems, medical systems and more. In addition to that, when we say, "*Let Your kingdom come, let Your will be done*", we're bringing His Kingdom (Heaven) from another dimension to earth! As co-laborers, we have a great amount of work ahead of us, and it must be done from heaven to earth! The question then remains: How do you establish and release a kingdom that you do not know? And how do you serve the interests of a king that you don't know? I believe if we understand what's rightfully ours as sons that question will finally be settled. We'll take an intimate look at this next.

PRIVILEGES, RIGHTS & RESPONSIBILITIES OF THE SONGS OF GOD

God has given us the ability to partner with Him to do amazing things. We are called to accomplish things in His kingdom we thought were relegated to superheroes and our imagination.

But, Ephesians 3:8-12 says this:

> [8] *To me, the very least of all saints, this grace was given, to preach to the Gentiles*
> *the unfathomable riches of Christ,* [9] *and to bring to light what is the administration*
> *of the mystery which for ages has been hidden in God who created all things;* [10] *so*
> *that the manifold wisdom of God might now be made known through the church to*
> *the rulers and the authorities in the heavenly places.* [11] *This was in accordance*
> *with the eternal purpose which He carried out in Christ Jesus our Lord,* [12] *in whom*
> *we have boldness and confident access through faith in Him.*

Isn't this amazing! Paul says he preached the riches of Christ to reveal the mysteries, hidden in God. The mysteries of Christ include our salvation, redemption and regeneration in Jesus, being born again from the Spirit Himself (John 3:6), being remade as new spirit beings (2 Corinthians 5:17), and the fact that God dwells on the inside of us (Romans 8)!

But why are these riches and mysteries of Christ revealed, according to Paul? It is so that the manifold wisdom of God might now be made known through the church to the rulers and the authorities in heavenly places. This means that through us, God will reveal His wisdom and as His wisdom is released, things move and change. We see from this scripture that we are meant to decree God's wisdom unknown to those in heaven and in the earth as rulers in heavenly places. We are meant to unleash the mind, the will and the way of God, thereby establishing His kingdom in heavenly places. By Holy Spirit, we shift the place of dominion back to the kingdom of God and from that place we decree the will of God in the earth.

Matthew 18:18-19 says this:

> [18] *Truly I say to you, whatever you bind on earth shall have been bound in heaven; and whatever you loose on earth shall have been loosed in heaven.*
> [19] *"Again I say to you, that if two of you agree on earth about anything that they may ask, it shall be done for them by My Father who is in heaven.*

This clearly portrays the authority we have in the heavens and the earth. In his book, Operating in the Courts of Heaven, Robert Henderson explains that binding and loosing are legal terms. To bind means to establish a binding agreement. To loose means to dissolve an existing contract.[xii]

Finally, Ephesians 6:10-12 states:

> [10] *Finally, be strong in the Lord and in the strength of His might.* [11] *Put on the full armor of God, so that you will be able to stand firm against the schemes of the*

devil. [12] For our struggle is not against flesh and blood, but against the rulers, against the powers, against the world forces of this darkness, against the spiritual forces of wickedness in the heavenly places.

As a child of God, we were created to declare the mysteries of God in heavenly places over rulers, powers and principalities of darkness that dominated areas meant for God's Kingdom. These places of dominion include our personal health, the destiny of our families, our jobs, cities, regions and even our nations. We are called to co-labor with God to dispossess these evil beings of their authority and to re-establish God's Kingdom in its place.

To do this, we need a deeper understanding of who we are as God's children. We must understand our privilege, right and responsibility as His children. Without the proper understanding we will fail to reach the full potential of who we are and exercise the authority we possess.

The Privilege of God's Children: Deep intimacy with God

The privilege of being a son of God is experiencing deep intimacy with God. He created us for His love. This leads us to a crucial point: Our identity is grounded in who we are to God! Our rulership is not based on what we do, but WHO WE ARE!

Paul, who arguably walked with God as deeply as any man could, prayed in Ephesians 3:14-19 that we would be strengthened in our inner man through faith. He prayed that we be rooted and grounded in God's love; having all wisdom, grace and strength to be intimately acquainted Him and overtaken by His love. He utters this prayer, after expounding upon the great mandate of making known the mysteries of God, to rulers in the heavens in verses 8 - 12.

So, considering our great calling as believers, we must be rooted and grounded, in His love. This foundation will prepare us to handle the power and weight of all He will release through us.

You see, for us to rule like Him, we must think like Him. And to think like Him we must know His heart. How do we get to know or understand the Father? Through INTIMACY. Intimacy with God allows us to constantly live experiences with Him. We need LIVE experiences of His love, the way He thinks, His desires and the how's and whys of what He wants to accomplish. These live experiences sync us with God. This synchronization is only one way we conform to His image. It's in His presence where our transformation into His likeness happens and we become an expression of His Love.

Romans 8:29-30 tells us:

> [29] *For those whom He foreknew, He also predestined to become conformed*
> *to the image of His Son, so that He would be the firstborn among many*
> *brethren;* [30] *and these whom He predestined, He also called; and these*
> *whom He called, He also justified; and these whom He justified, He also*
> *glorified.*

As we spend time in worship, we are conformed into the likeness of Jesus. We become more and more like our Elder brother. He came to show us the Father and reveal the Kingdom. It stands to reason, for us to know how to walk out the Kingdom of God we must follow the example of the Son of God who perfectly fulfilled the Father's will.

Despite popular belief, God is enjoyable and a delight. He wants to share all of who He is with us. And in the sharing of our weaknesses, frailties, misunderstandings, immaturity etc. we exchange these things for more of God. It's the place of intimacy with God where we humble ourselves and decrease and God in His power, might and magnificence increases and we are unified with Him.

2 Corinthians 3:17-18 says, *"Now the Lord is the Spirit, and where the Spirit of the Lord is, there is liberty. But we all, with unveiled face, beholding as in a mirror the glory of the Lord, are being transformed into the same image from glory to glory, just as from the Lord, the Spirit."*

Here, Paul is referencing Moses' experience with the Glory of God in Exodus 33:12-13. Moses asked God to see His glory. God responded I would cause my goodness to pass before you and I will proclaim my name to you. However, you (Moses) will not see my face. God hid Moses in the cleft of a rock as He passed by. He covered Moses until He had passed so that Moses could only see His back. The power of that encounter caused an amazing outcome. God's glory radiated from Moses' face after that encounter though Moses did not see God's face. As the glory of God from Moses encounter with Him began to fade, Moses covered his face in embarrassment.

In 2 Corinthians 3:17-18, Paul is explaining that Jesus tore the veil that prevented us from having full access to God and the revelation of His kingdom. Unlike Moses, we need not be concerned with the glory of God fading from us. If we abide in Him, it will only increase. We get to behold God with an unveiled face, seeing His glory and being transformed by it. Transformation is a benefit of our intimacy with God. It comes as we position ourselves in a place to meet with Him and get to know Him.

Paul's writings were directly to the Church, the body of Christ. This means that the privilege of intimacy with God is reserved just for us!

Ephesians 2:4-10 tells us,

> *4But God, being rich in mercy, because of His great love with which He loved us, 5even when we were dead in our transgressions, made us alive together with Christ (by grace you have been saved), 6and raised us up with Him, and seated us with Him in the heavenly places in Christ Jesus,*

[7] so that in the ages to come He might show the surpassing riches of His grace in kindness toward us in Christ Jesus. [8] For by grace you have been saved through faith; and that not of yourselves, it is the gift of God; 9 not as a result of works, so that no one may boast. 10 For we are His workmanship, created in Christ Jesus for good works, which God prepared beforehand so that we would walk in them.

As we worship God, beholding his beauty and glory, we are transformed into His image. This transformation prepares us for the good works He has prepared for us.

The Right of God's Children: Inheritance of the Kingdom

As God's children, we have an inheritance in Him. All things belong to God and are subject to His reign. He has extended that realm to earth and given us the ability to rule as Him.

Through our resurrection in Jesus, we are now seated in heaven in Christ above all rulers, authorities and principalities. This means that the things that are under His feet, i.e. subject to His dominion, are also under our feet. Ephesians 2:4-6 is the perfect example of this truth. In verses 1 through 3 Paul explains how we were all once dead in our trespasses, living according to the lusts of the flesh and in complete disobedience to God, and then a transformation happens,

"[4]But God, being rich in mercy, because of His great love with which He loved us, [5]even when we were dead in our transgressions, made us alive together with Christ (by grace you have been saved), [6]and raised us up with Him, and seated us with Him in the heavenly places in Christ Jesus, [7]so that in the ages to come He might show the surpassing riches of His grace in kindness toward us in Christ Jesus. [8]For by grace you have been saved through faith; and that not of yourselves, it is the gift of God; [9]not as a result of works, so that no one may boast. [10]For we are His workmanship,

created in Christ Jesus for good works, which God prepared beforehand so that we would walk in them."

Our resurrection in Christ comes once we chose to become a part of God's family by accepting Jesus as our Savior, acknowledging Him as God and King. Recognizing our need for His work on the cross for our redemption. We also receive the precious gift of Holy Spirit as a part of our inheritance and a guarantee of God's inheritance in us.

Ephesians 1:13-14 explains, *"13 In Him (Jesus), you also, after listening to the message of truth, the gospel of your salvation—having also believed, you were sealed in Him with the Holy Spirit of promise, 14 who is given as a pledge of our inheritance, with a view to the redemption of God's own possession, to the praise of His glory."* We also receive several spiritual gifts that empower us to live supernaturally and establish heaven on earth. These gifts include healing, faith, prophesy, administration, service, discerning of spirits, heightened wisdom, and the list goes on (see Romans 12, 1 Corinthians 12, Ephesians 4)!

And just after this, Ephesians 1:19-23 explains that the Father seated Christ at His right hand in heavenly places, "*far above all rule and authority and power and dominion, and every name that is named*, (NASB)". Since we are a part of the body of Christ, we are now seated in heavenly places and these powers are under our feet as well. If we remain in alignment with the will of God, all things are under our rule and dominion, through Christ.

When we became a part of the family of God, our inheritance of rulership was waiting for us. And through our redemption, we can now walk in the good works God preordained us to walk in. Guys, we have an inheritance of a seat, a position of rulership, in God's Kingdom! God has prepared the works, duties, responsibilities and positions of rulership prior to our acceptance of Jesus.

Yes, growth is necessary. Yes, maturity is required. These are necessary elements for us to walk out the fullness of that inheritance. Do not worry! Remember, even Jesus had to learn. Luke 2:52 tells us that Jesus grew in wisdom and stature with God and men. Simply put, we are not exempt from the processing that's required in our journey with God. If Jesus, being the son of God, was held to that standard, then so are we...As Jesus said to the apostles in John 14.12 that they would do even greater works than He did. The promises of God are an inheritance of the children of God, so expect to do greater!

Remember, we were created through Christ to do good works. All that we do in His kingdom should be for His kingdom!

Responsibility of God's Children: Take Dominion in the Earth to Establish His Kingdom

As the sons of God, we are responsible to rule take our position in Christ and complete the good works that God pre-ordained for us to do. It is our position of sonship that brought us into rulership. We have a place of authority in God's kingdom because we are His children through Christ. We rule because we are sons, we are not sons because we rule.

Our Genesis objective to have dominion over the earth never changed. Through Jesus, our ability to fulfill this objective according to the will of God has been reinstated. We are new creatures in Christ, the old has passed away and we are made new beings 2 Corinthians 5:17).

According to Galatians 2:19-21, *"[19]For through the Law I died to the Law, so that I might live to God. [20]I have been crucified with Christ; and it is no longer I who live, but Christ lives in me; and the life which I now live in the flesh I live by faith in the Son of God, who loved me and gave Himself up for me. [21]I do not nullify the grace of God, for if righteousness comes through the Law, then Christ died needlessly."*

We see here that we find our life solely through Jesus, not through what we do. We are made righteous because He is righteous, and we are now found in Him. If we are found in Him, we live as He lives, think as He thinks and rule as He rules.

Fulfilling our destinies, obtaining our inheritance and serving those to whom we are called is God's expectation of us as His children, it is not an option. As His children, it is our great responsibility to live out the destiny that God ordained for us. In doing so we will save lives, build lives, change systems, dismantle darkness and establish the culture of the Kingdom of Heaven on the earth.

You see, there is a cost to be a co-laborer with Christ. The cost is "not my will but your will be done." It's dying to our will and desires, and relinquishing control to the plans of God. I once had a conversation with a good friend concerning an area I was with struggling. My heart's desire was to follow God's will and wait for His promise of marriage. But my flesh desired to supersede God and decide. A decision I knew would only make me happy in the now. I lacked vision for the moment that God would shift my life to bring the person I could marry. Of course, this was not the first time I had this dilemma. My friend said something profound that settled my heart. Essentially, it was this: you're human and you have feelings, but you are doing what you can do. Holy Spirit gave you instructions and you are following them. Your flesh is telling you one thing, but you are saying "not my will but your will be done. That's all you can do, and you leave the rest to God."

We all experience these moments: moments where we are living out what it means to identify with Christ's sufferings. But after we've suffered awhile, there's an opportunity to share in His glory. Jesus Himself struggled with the cross and asked the Father to let the cup pass from Him. In the end, He chose the way of the Father, the way of the cross. Now you and I are alive with the promise of a life beyond our dreams and in the family of the God of the Universe.

The gifts of the Spirit (prophecy, healing, administration, miracles, acts of services, faith, and more) were given to build something, the Kingdom of God. Let's not waste our talents any further but take up the call as co-laborers and advance the kingdom!

---

[x] https://wol.jw.org/en/wol/d/r1/lp-e/1200003064
[xi] https://www.merriam-webster.com/dictionary/kingdom
[xii] Henderson, Robert. Operating in the Courts of Heaven, pg. 45-47

Chapter 4 Review Questions

1. What was the nobleman's expectation of his servants while he was away on his journey in the parable in Luke 19?
2. What is the definition of a co-laborer?
3. What is the privilege of a child of God?
4. What is the right of a child of God?
5. What is the responsibility of a child of God?

Chapter 5: Generals In The Kingdom

Oftentimes the term "general" is used to describe someone who was a major leader in a movement or organization. For example, Martin Luther King was a general in the Civil Rights Movement. Definitively, a general is a military term that describes an officer in the highest (1st-3rd) ranks. Ecclesiastically, it is used to refer to the chief official of a religious order. Being a general clearly has to do with rank, authority, and leadership. So, the title "God's General" is indicative of someone who has a high rank in the Kingdom of God, along with the authority and leadership that cause them to bring the Kingdom of God into the Earth. Roberts Liardon, who spent a significant portion of his life researching these types of people, coined the term "God's General."

Roberts had an encounter with the Lord at 12 years old. In this encounter, God instructed him to study the lives of great men and women of God. During his study, he would learn of their successes and their failures, and it would become an important part of his training for ministry. He started his research immediately after this visitation. Even at the young age of 12 he took his studying very seriously. He would read every book he could get his hands on about moves of God. He even researched the men and women until he found them or their closest relatives. God granted Roberts favor with the generals he was studying. They would allow him to interview them and eventually started building relationships with him, too. People would give him their artifacts, pictures and books, which are all now on display at his bible college. He finished his research at age 16 and began preaching, publishing his book, God's Generals, later in his life[13].

Highlighting God's Generals displays the importance of partnering with the Lord to achieve supernatural Kingdom success in the earth. It shows us that this level of co-laboring - working together with the Lord - is not only a realistic goal, but it is also an attainable one for us as Sons of God. These are people that partnered with God in the supernatural, causing them to accomplish things that they never would have been able to without Him.

Below, I highlight some of the key Generals who have impacted the body of Christ. This is not an exhaustive list. There are other great and notable Generals. However, these Generals display the supernatural life of God, a key element of operating in Heaven's government.

MARIA WOODWORTH-ETTER (1844-1924)

Maria was known for demonstrating the Spirit of God in the late 1800s and is thought to have paved the way for the Pentecostal movements that came after her ministry. She had a vision in which angels came into her room and took her across the country. Jesus then told her that people would fall as she preached. This vision pushed her to answer the call of God on her life.[14] Once she started preaching, her ministry grew exponentially in a very short time frame. Thousands of people were saved at her meetings. Her meetings were known for people being "struck down as dead men" into trances. The power of the Spirit was so heavy during her meetings that people were said to fall into these same trances miles away. They would always get up having had such a powerful experience with God that they immediately made Him their Lord and Savior[2].

In 1885, so many were saved in one city that the police said they had nothing to do because so much had changed[2]. Thousands more were saved as a result of seeing the radical healings that took place. In a meeting of 25,000, hundreds of people were overtaken by the power of God before she ever finished preaching. She preached that these strong manifestations of the Spirit were "nothing new; they were just something that the Church has lost[2]." She only desired for the Holy Spirit to do His works and for His gifts to manifest as He saw fit. She was the only leading evangelist of the Holiness movement who embraced the Pentecostal experience of speaking in tongues. This was pivotal during a time that many ministers didn't understand the manifestations of the Holy Spirit.

She lived in the realm of the Spirit as a powerful vessel of God's divine leading and His supernatural manifestations. A key to her ministry was the spiritual authority she gained through disciplining herself in intercession and staying fervent in prayer until heaven was open. She would simply raise her hands and everyone there would feel the power of Holy Spirit, with people being healed in that very moment[2]. Every manner of sickness and disease that showed up at her meetings bowed itself to Jesus Christ and was disintegrated by the fire of the Spirit.

Her spiritual legacy can be witnessed through many Pentecostal denominations, including Foursquare[2]. Smith Wigglesworth is believed to have been a disciple of her ministry. E.W. Kenyon was one as well, going on to found Bethel Bible School and to have a great healing and teaching ministry[2]. Aimee Semple McPherson is thought to have received her mantle.

Her great-great-great grandson said, "The thing that impressed him most was how completely her life was sold out to God. She was unlike so many today. She went wherever God told her to go, whether they had 20 people or a thousand people. Her time belonged to God. She was never too busy to do what He said. Everyone was important to her because they were important to God. That is why she knew God so well. That is why she could punch someone in the stomach or whack him or her in the neck. She knew God and she knew He would heal them."[2]

WILLIAM SEYMOUR (1870-1922)

Roberts Liardon refers to William Seymour as the catalyst to Pentecost. The baptism of the Holy Spirit with the evidence of speaking in tongues was a major part of the revival he led.

He became the leader of the first organized movement that promoted the Pentecostal experience, the Azusa Street Revival. Seymour preached and passionately believed in the baptism of the Holy Spirit solely through speaking in tongues even before he had received the baptism himself. During this time, the early 1900s, this was a very controversial teaching even in the Holiness denominations. One minister later said, "The contention was all on our part. I have never met a man who had such control over his spirit. No amount of confusion and accusation seemed to disturb him. He would sit behind that packing case and smile at us until we were all condemned by our own activities.[15]"

He began to hold prayer meetings regularly at a home, earnestly seeking the baptism of the Holy Spirit. The leaders would pray all night together for one another's deliverance, believing the word and not stopping until they saw its manifestation. They put a demand on the authority of the Word of God. Once, they even commanded insects that were killing crops to stay outside of certain boundaries, and the insects obeyed[16]. After some time spent fasting, the Holy Spirit fell on those in the house and into the neighborhood just like on the day of Pentecost. People were falling out for hours in trances under the power of the Spirit. On the 3rd day, Seymour himself was filled with the Holy Spirit. The movement quickly outgrew the house where they were meeting.

This led to them moving into the legendary building on Azusa Street in April 1906. Seymour held fast to his belief and discipline in spending hours praying in tongues and seeking the Lord. These meetings were spontaneous: they could last for hours or days and sometimes, entire sermons were given by tongues and interpretation[4]. But the people never tired, saying the Holy Spirit energized them. The presence of the Lord was so tangible that it caused the people to ascribe to a higher standard of living. They began to live in holiness and grew in manifesting the divine love of God amongst each other so as not to grieve the Spirit of God. The fear of the Lord gripped people outside of the building and His presence was so heavy people would drop in the streets and get up speaking in tongues[4]! The fire department was even called because people thought the roof was on fire, but it was the Glory of God manifesting!

So many unusual and instantaneous miracles happened during the time of the Azusa Street Revival that all of them could not be recorded. The crowds grew to thousands of people, overtaking and surrounding the building. Missionaries were birthed and launched from Azusa, carrying the Pentecostal message around the world. Aimee Semple McPherson planted her ministry in LA because of this movement[4]. Many Pentecostal denominations also attribute their founding to the participants of Azusa. These denominations include the Assemblies of God, the Pentecostal Assemblies of the World, and the Full Gospel Businessmen's Fellowship. There is so much of William's legacy still in the earth today, all because of his commitment to the Holy Spirit and His supernatural power.

JOHN G. LAKE (1870-1935)

John G. Lake had an amazing healing ministry. He said his one goal was to bring the fullness of God to every person, believing that every Spirit-filled believer should enjoy the same type of ministry Jesus did while living on earth[17]. He believed this reality could only be accomplished by seeing ourselves as God sees us. The spirits of death and infirmity gripped his family, but he believed in healing despite these circumstances, taking several of his siblings to John Alexander Dowie's healing rooms to be healed. His wife also struggled with sickness for years until the point she found herself on her deathbed. It was at this point that he truly grasped the revelation that satan was the author of sickness and death. After declaring her to be healed and calling upon God, the power of God overtook her causing paralysis to leave and her heartbeat to normalize. Her coughing ceased, her breathing regulated and her temperature normalized, too. Her healing became national news, thrusting them both into a highly sought after healing ministry[18].

People came to their home from all over to be healed. John spoke of the anointing of God's Spirit flowing through him like electricity, stating that there are laws of the Spirit just like there are laws of electricity. He had learned to walk in the Spirit in a way he described like this: "It became easy for me to detach myself from the course of life so that while my hands and mind were engaged in the common affairs of every day, my spirit maintained its attitude of communion with God.[6]" In 1906, he began to pray for the baptism of the Holy Spirit, receiving it months later while praying for a sick woman stating, "When the phenomena of it had passed, the glory of it remained in my soul. I found that my life began to manifest a varied range of the gifts of the Spirit. And I spoke in tongues by the power of God, and God flowed through me with a new force. Healings were of a more powerful order[6]."

His ministry changed dynamically after this experience with God. He said that he had healed hundreds of people before it, but healed thousands after it expressing that "tongues have been, to me, the making of my ministry. It is that peculiar communication with God that reveals to my soul the truth I utter to you day by day in the ministry[6]."

He soon began ministry in Africa. Hundreds receiving the baptism of the Holy Spirit along with massive healings distinguished his meetings. Within one year he started 100 churches[6]. When a plague started moving through the country, killing thousands, he and his team would remove the dead bodies but never got sick. As he was questioned about this, he invited the doctors to do an experiment on him by placing some of the active plague on his hand, assuring them that the cells would die immediately. The doctor found this to be true after watching it happen under a microscope. Lake reinforced his message of the gospel by proclaiming "It is the law of the Spirit of life in Christ Jesus. I believe that just as long as I keep my soul in contact with the living God so that His Spirit is flowing into my soul and body, that no germ will ever attach itself to me, for the Spirit of God will kill it[6]." This is the power that flowed through his hands into the bodies of those for whose healing he prayed.

Several of God's Generals, including Maria Woodworth-Etter and William Seymour, influenced him. Quotes can be found of him discussing how he would pray like Mother Etter prayed to let the Spirit move through him and how Seymour's words spoke to his spirit. His ministry efforts in Africa produced much fruit after only 5 years: 1250 preachers, 625 congregations, 100K converts, and countless miracles[6]. He established healing rooms in Spokane, Washington, where it is estimated that 100,000 healings took place (many of which are recorded). Between the years of 1915-1920, Spokane was deemed the "healthiest city in the world" because of his ministry, with the mayor honoring his efforts[6]. His daughter described him as having "a very great consciousness of being a king and priest before God, showing a bearing and dominion of that nobility[6]." This can be seen from his ministry and legacy to this day.

Although these are just a few examples of God's Generals, it is easy to think that because of the time periods in which they lived and ministered that their legacy did not continue or isn't present today. However, this is not true. While it may not be mainstream, there are still modern day God's Generals and movements, some of which are alive and well today.

MAMA MARY JENKINS (1909-2011)

Mary was a spiritual daughter of Smith Wigglesworth. He prophesied about her to her father when she was only 3 years old. He anointed her at the age of 7 and brought her into an apprenticeship on the road with him when she was 20 years of age. Smith told her that her ministry wouldn't truly begin until she was in her sixties and that was a fact[19]. After her apprenticeship, she went on to marry a bishop of 7 churches, have children, conduct a choir, and enjoy singing with her cousin, Mahalia Jackson. However, she never stopped being visited by angels and delivering accurate prophetic words throughout this time period.

She had a life and death experience at 62 years old and was raised from the dead in a hospital. This immediately launched her ministry, which was abundant with miracles and signs of the Spirit. She raised over 27 babies from the dead, taking them out of their coffins and handing them back to their parents[7]. She walked into a morgue and brought a corpse back to life to attend his own funeral. In New England, Mama Mary emptied an entire mental health facility simply by walking in[7]. All the patients were instantly healed causing the hospital to close shortly thereafter. Once, she followed the leading of the Lord out of state until she arrived at a hospital and overheard the staff talking about a set of Siamese twins. She found the parents and separated the children by calling on the Lord, leaving everyone dumbfounded. Mary was known for stopping bank robberies, emptying bars, and she even converted a motorcycle gang that tried to rob her[7]! They confessed Jesus as their Savior with several going on to become preachers. She was a woman of faith and carrier of the presence of God. These attributes gave her the authority to do amazing things seemingly effortlessly.

HEIDI BAKER (1959-present)

Heidi began a new ministry to focus on abandoned children by moving to Mozambique with her husband in 1995. Soon after, she contracted tuberculosis and pneumonia. She went to a healing meeting where she had a vision of Jesus telling her there would always be enough for her to take care of the children because of his sacrifice on the cross. She was healed after this. Their ministry has become known for the miraculous, even having a medical journal publish verifiable evidence of visual and hearing improvements in people who had received prayer from the ministry[20]. More than 100 people have been raised from the dead and food is regularly multiplied[21]. Along with these miracles, the deaf, blind and crippled are being restored as the gospel is spread through these nations. Her ministry expanded from owning a former government orphanage to operating free health clinics, primary and secondary schools, village feeding programs, cottage industries and over 10,000 churches becoming affiliated with her ministry, Iris Global[22]. She believes the beatitudes are God's recipe for revival stating, "When we walk as Jesus walked, we will be blessed. Jesus meant that poor in spirit is a posturing of the heart where one is wholly given, fully yielded, completely desperate, and totally dependent on God alone.[23]" This intimacy is what causes the Kingdom to show up daily in their midst and her ministry to continue to thrive.

BETHEL MINISTRIES (1996-present)

While the original Bethel Church was established in the 1950s, it shifted when Bill Johnson became the pastor in 1996[24]. He came in with a mindset to pursue revival, and the outpouring of the Holy Spirit began almost immediately. They saw many healings and miracles, including testimonies of cancer disappearing[25]. The healings and miracles, along with the heavy atmosphere of worship they have cultivated, have become their norm, causing people to travel there from all over the world to receive life-changing encounters with God. The church has established healing rooms and a school of supernatural ministry that teaches people how to flow in the supernatural and miraculous. It is here that they promote and teach a dependency on the presence of God with an emphasis on the Holy Spirit's flow and His impartation[13]. Bill believes that valuing the presence of God and believing that the supernatural activity of the Bible is still available for us today is what causes things to happen at Bethel[12]. This is the mindset in which the ministry imparts as it trains people to begin standing in their rightful places as the Body of Christ for the expansion of the Kingdom.

MORE OF GOD'S GENERALS

This list is not at all exhaustive. In fact, it only includes brief details about many of their lives. There is much more information available about how the supernatural manifested in these people's lives through their willingness to co-labor with God, bringing the dominion of His Kingdom into the earth. The significant level of manifestation of the Kingdom that they experienced, along with the weight of the glory of God that they carried, is what qualifies them to be called God's Generals. It is impossible to achieve this without substantial spiritual rank, authority and leadership in the Kingdom of God. All of which is born through and sustained by the depth and intimacy of their relationships with God. The same is true for every Spirit-filled believer.

Here is a list of more of God's Generals for greater study and understanding of our ability and responsibility to partner with the Lord to achieve His will in the earth.

1. John Alexander Dowie (1847-1907) – Scottish Evangelist & Healing Apostle
2. Charles F. Parham (1873-1929) – Pentecostal Leader
3. Smith Wigglesworth (1859-1947) – Apostle of Healing & Faith
4. Evan Roberts (1878-1951) – Welsh Revivalist
5. Aimee Semple Mcpherson (1890-1944) – Pentecostal Evangelist
6. Kathryn Kuhlman (1907-1976) – Hand Maiden of the Holy Spirit
7. William Branham (1909-1965) – Healing Revivalist
8. A. A. Allen (1911-1970) – Healing & Deliverance Evangelist
9. Jack Coe (1918-1956) – Faith Healer
10. Billy Graham (1918-2018) – Pentecostal Evangelist
11. Arturo Skinner (1924-1975) – Apostle of Deliverance
12. Frances Metcalfe – Harp & Bowl Ministry, Founder of the Golden Candlestick
13. Ana Mendez Ferrell (1954-present) – Apostolic Deliverance Minister
14. James Maloney (~1950s-present) – Miraculous Apostle

---

[13] Liardon, Roberts. God's Generals: Why They Succeeded and Why Some Failed. 1997. Pages 13-14
[14] Liardon, Roberts. God's Generals: Why They Succeeded and Why Some Failed. 1997. Pages 45-63
[15] Liardon, Roberts. God's Generals: Why They Succeeded and Why Some Failed. 1997. Page 130
[16] Liardon, Roberts. God's Generals: Why They Succeeded and Why Some Failed. 1997. Pages 126-148
[17] Liardon, Roberts. God's Generals: Why They Succeeded and Why Some Failed. 1997. Page 153
[18] Liardon, Roberts. God's Generals: Why They Succeeded and Why Some Failed. 1997. Pages 151-174
[19] Jones Manuel, Dr. Shelli. Remembering Mary Mama Jenkins, https://borntopray.wordpress.com/2011/11/30/remembering-mary-mama-jenkins/

[20] Brown, Candy Gunther; Mory, Stephen C.; Williams, Rebecca; McClymond, Michael J. (2010). "Study of the Therapeutic Effects of Proximal Intercessory Prayer (STEPP) on Auditory and Visual Impairments in Rural Mozambique". *Southern Medical Journal.* **103** (9): 864–869.

[21] Stafford, Tim. "Miracles in Mozambique: How Mama Heidi Reaches the Abandoned." Christianity Today, https://www.christianitytoday.com/ct/2012/may/miracles-in-mozambique.html

[22] Iris Global Website, https://www.irisglobal.org/about/history

[23] Biswell, Christy. "Heidi Baker: Intimacy for Miracles." Christian Broadcasting Network, http://www1.cbn.com/700club/heidi-baker-intimacy-miracles

[24] Johnson, Bill. http://bjm.org/bill/

[25] Winters, Amanda. Faith Healings, Dead Raising Teams Part of Bethel Experience. http://archive.redding.com/news/faith-healings-dead-raising-teams-part-of-bethel-experience-ep-377152376-355396981.html/

CHAPTER 5 REVIEW QUESTIONS

1. What is a General in the Kingdom?
2. What was a key to Maria Etter-Woodworth's ministry?
3. What was the primary experience being emphasized that lead to Pentecost being poured out in the United States?
4. What did John G. Lake say was the making of his ministry? Why?
5. What two attributes of Mama Mary Jenkins gave her the authority to do what she did?

SECTION II: CO-LABORERS QUIZ

1.) Please explain the term 'co-laborer'.

____

____

____

2.) Please tell why co-laborers are so important in the Kingdom of God.

____

____

____

3.) A General in the Kingdom is ... (Please pick one answer)

a. A person of High rank who walks in authority & supernatural power within the Kingdom of God
b. The Captain of the Host
c. One who is apart of the Angelic Army of God
d. A Five-Fold minister

4.) Please name some of the characteristics of a General in the Kingdom?

____

____

____

5.) What was the key similarity between the Azusa Street Revival and the Day of Pentecost? (Please pick one answer)

a. The time of day
b. Baptism of Holy Spirit, evidence of speaking in tongues
c. Men and Women took part in this experience
d. Both Revivals were held in small facilities

6.) Please choose one of the Generals in the Kingdom and explain in 3-5 sentences what type of impact they had or have on the Kingdom.

____

____

____

____

7.) John G. Lake... (Please pick one answer)

e. Assisted William Seymour in the Asuza Street Revival
f. Turned 100 years old then died of old age
g. Moved to Ohio to start churches under the Assembly of God Organizations.
h. Established healing rooms in Spokane, Washington estimating over 100,000 healings on record

8. Please explain how the Baptism of Holy Spirit impacted the life and ministry of John. G. Lake.

____
____
____

9.) Mama Mary Jenkins was the spiritual daughter of... (Please pick one answer)

i. John G. Lake
j. Smith Wigglesworth
k. Alexander Dowie
l. A. A. Allen

10.) Mama Mary Jenkins raised _______ babies from the dead, taking them from their coffins. She also stopped ________________ ________________ and converted a whole motorcycle ____________________. (Please fill in the blanks)

11.) Please explain why Bethel Ministries experiences so many Heavenly encounters, signs, wonders and miracles.

____
____
____

Section III: The Anatomy of The Courts of Heaven

Chapter 6: Introduction to the Courts of Heaven

6For a child will be born to us, a son will be given to us;
And the government will rest on His shoulders;
And His name will be called Wonderful Counselor, Mighty God,
Eternal Father, Prince of Peace.
7There will be no end to the increase of His government or of peace,
On the throne of David and over his kingdom,
To establish it and to uphold it with justice and righteousness
From then on and forevermore.
The zeal of the Lord of hosts will accomplish this.
- Isaiah 9:6-7

To understand the courts of Heaven and their existence, we must first understand God as our Father. We are taught to see God in many ways (Provider, Warrior, Miracle Worker, Savior, etc.) however, seeing Him as Father often eludes us. It is possible that our inability to relate to God as a Father stems from what is lacking in our natural father/child relationships. It is imperative to know that God is not like man. His attributes as a Father is: He is a good Father, full of love who desires deep and intimate relationship with us. As I came before God in prayer to write this chapter, Jesus took my hand and led me to the throne of God. Upon entering, the Father presented a necklace to me as a gift. The necklace was His way of demonstrating how moved He was by perseverance and continued to serve Him even through my failures… that happen often.

This is an example of the Father to whom we belong, the One who desires to know us and for us to know Him. He does not disapprove of me because I fail sometimes. He encouraged my persistence and affirmed me, as needed. And this is the good Father who created us to do good works for His Kingdom. Sounds good, doesn't it? However, I must emphasize that these good works are not devoid of Him, but are completed with Him in His Kingdom. Understanding this: that He is God and His way is the only way. We must be willing to deny ourselves, i.e. our flesh, fears, misunderstandings, rights, etc., and follow Him. God's way is not only the only way, IT is the best way to live.

A VISION OF HIS LOVE

During one of our many court sessions, I had the following vision. It expanded my understanding of how much God loves us and how important it is to Him that we participate in reigning with Him in His kingdom. In the vision, Jesus returned to Heaven after His resurrection and leaving the disciples on earth. I watched Him, as He quickly walked into a massive courtroom. The room was very beautiful. The entire room, including the walls, floors and furnishings, was a warm, cream-colored stone. At the entrance were double doors that led to a wide hallway with the same cream-colored stone. Jesus flung open the doors to the courtroom then sat in a chair, legs crossed, and waited. But no one came into the room, and He's been waiting ever since. But who or what was Jesus waiting on? As I saw this vision I knew Jesus was waiting on us!

Remember when Jesus said, *"Do not let your heart be troubled; believe in God, believe also in Me. In My Father's house are many dwelling places; if it were not so, I would have told you; for I go to prepare a place for you. If I go and prepare a place for you, I will come again and receive you to Myself, that where I am, there you may be also. And you know the way where I am going,* (John 14:1-4)."

Why was he waiting on us? He was patiently waiting for His redeemed ones to take their position and begin operating within the government of Heaven. There is a position of governance and influence available as we begin to take our place in His courts and intercede for His will to be done in the earth. We are to exercise our authority through His blood; to remove the legalities of the enemy's accusation. This is one of the places Jesus has prepared for us, in His Kingdom. It's a place of rulership and governance within His courts. Now the invitation was extended, and He is patiently waiting. As the vision progressed people began to trickle in and Jesus' face lit up. There was no condemnation. He wasn't upset or angry, but full of love and welcoming. In that moment, I saw Him as an exemplary teacher and a good King. He gathered those who came as if no time had passed, led them into the courtroom, then through another door. From there they began one of the best journeys of their lives.

Jesus has extended this invitation to us. I, for one, would not leave Him waiting. I mean it's Jesus! Who would pass up such an invitation?! Let's go on this journey with Him, having the faith and courage to step into something new in God. This step will take us on a transformational journey and we will discover we were meant to be: The manifested sons of God, purposefully establishing His Kingdom on the earth. Our hope is that through knowing this vision, you will feel the love that the Father, Holy Spirit, and Jesus have for you and their desire to see you come into your place of rulership in the Kingdom. Now, from this place let's look further at the government of Heaven and its systems.

HEAVEN'S GOVERNMENT & THE REALITY OF THE COURTS

The concept of the courts of Heaven is a foundational part of operating in the government of Heaven. When we operate in the courts, we address accusations of the enemy and his cohorts presented against us before God. These accusations prevent the release of God's Kingdom on earth and perpetuate the reign of the kingdom of darkness. When we properly administrate the will of God through Heaven's court system, accusations are dismantled. After accusations are addressed, God pronounces the verdict(s) in our favor. The verdict gives us His authority to make decrees that shift the affairs of our lives, cities, regions and nations. How amazing is that? Like in the earthly court system, in the courts of Heaven we can bring petitions and address accusations to court. This gives us the authority necessary to abolish the hold of the enemy and establish verdicts in favor of God's will.

In Christendom, especially in America, we have become unfamiliar with the supernatural and dependent on our intellect and our flesh to interpret scripture. We are ignorant about how to engage with the reality of the supernatural. We read the Word of God and interpret the fantastic, supernatural passages to be symbolic, as a representation of sorts, or label them "for another time and not for this day." I can testify that I was one who thought this way prior to my growth in relationship with Holy Spirit, the Revealer of all Truth (John 16:14-15). Holy Spirit expanded and increased my spiritual sensitivity in profound ways. He taught me how to hear, sense, and feel God in a way that is beyond my intellect. At that point of transition in my life, I came to the revelation that God is tangible. His Kingdom and the courts of Heaven are also tangible.

The Courts of Heaven are real; they exist as a reality in the spiritual realm of Heaven. **They. Are. Real**. When I was first introduced to this revelation, I had no prior knowledge or exposure to it. Being a pew baby – born and raised in church – for people like me, new revelations can be jarring. After spending decades in the church, one would assume that all principles would be uncovered – at least in a general sense, right? Unfortunately, that assumption is quite false. Whether it is from our personal denominational experiences or a limited belief system, we must remain teachable and open to new revelations from the Holy Spirit. The facts that mysteries are released in different time periods or dispensations (Ephesians 1:7-12) and God's ways are higher than ours and beyond our human comprehension should help us remain this way. There is an overabundance of reasons why this should be our heart posture towards Holy Spirit. The Holy Spirit is important to highlight here because God is one with His word (John 1:1) and He will not contradict Himself. Whenever we have an issue with reconciling the word of God, it is indicative of our limited understanding and humanity. It's by no means failure on the part of our all-knowing God. Therefore, the Spirit of Truth – Holy Spirit – will only point back to Himself using the truth of God and contextually accurate scriptures.

"Beloved, do not believe every spirit [speaking through a self-proclaimed prophet]; instead test the spirits to see whether they are from God, because many false prophets and teachers have gone out into the world. [2] By this you know and recognize the Spirit of God: every spirit that acknowledges and confesses [the fact] that Jesus Christ has [actually] come in the flesh [as a man] is from God [God is its source]; [3] and every spirit that does not confess Jesus [acknowledging that He has come in the flesh, but would deny any of the Son's true nature] is not of God; this is the spirit of the antichrist, which you have heard is coming, and is now already in the world."
1 John 4:1-3

This is a key principle when it comes to discerning the spirit behind any new revelation. It is a principle that my natural father taught me to value. As I dug deeper into the concept of the courts of Heaven, this scriptural foundation was a great help in deciphering this newfound revelation. I was also in a place where I was asking the Lord what my prayer life was missing. I believed that my prayers were in alignment with His word and will for my life, but yet they remained unanswered. How could this be?!?! So, the revelation of the courts of Heaven was very much an answered prayer for me. It is my belief it will be the same for many believers reading this book.

So, let's dig into this topic a bit further. Just as the throne of God is a real place, His courts are a real place. Because of Jesus' sacrifice, the veil was torn, and those who accept Him as Lord and Savior have access to these places in their daily lives. I cannot emphasize enough that the courts of Heaven ARE a real place, in Heaven! Selah! It is important that this fact is understood because of the weight and authority that operating in the courts carries: It is a part of the Kingdom's Heavenly governmental system. In the same way you wouldn't take going to US Court lightly, you should not take going to the Heavenly Court lightly. In fact, I would venture to say Heaven's court system weighs more because it is where the ultimate Judge resides.

By definition, a court is a place where justice is administered. Jesus, Himself, places prayer in the courtroom in the parable of the widow and the judge (Luke 18:1-8). This is made more apparent when we examine the basic definition of prayer, which is a petition unto God. Now, this definition may seem simple enough, but we often overlook the fact that the word petition is a legal term. A petition is defined as a formally drawn request that is addressed to a person (or people) in authority or power, soliciting some favor, right, mercy or other benefit; it is an application for a court order or for some judicial action[26]. With that said, let's look at the parable from this perspective:

"*Then He spoke a parable to them, that men always ought to pray and not lose heart, [2] saying: "There was in a certain city a judge who did not fear God nor regard man. [3] Now there was a widow in that city; and she came to him, saying, 'Get justice for me from my adversary.' [4] And he would not for a while; but afterward he said within himself, 'Though I do not fear God nor regard man, [5] yet because this widow troubles me I will avenge her, lest by her continual coming she weary me.'" [6] Then the Lord said, "Hear what the unjust judge said. [7] And shall God not avenge His own elect who cry out day and night to Him, though He bears long with them? [8] I tell you that He will avenge them speedily. Nevertheless, when the Son of Man comes, will He really find faith on the earth?"* Luke 18:1-8

The purpose of this parable was to emphasize that we "*always ought to pray and not lose heart*". To make this more practical and gain further insight we must fully embrace the principle at work: repeated petitions to a judge. We know that God is the final and ultimate judge. Many people, whether they claim Christ or not, admit to the fact that God is the judge. However, many of us who follow Christ, fail to apply this principle to our lives when we neglect to seek Him as the Judge.

"*God is a just judge, and God is angry with the wicked every day.*" Psalms 7:11

"*For the Lord is our judge, The Lord is our Lawgiver, The Lord is our King; He will save us.*" Isaiah 33:22

"*But we know that the judgment of God is according to truth against those who practice such things.*" Romans 2:2

"*For it is time for judgment to begin with the household of God; and if it begins with us first, what will be the outcome for those that do not obey the gospel of God?"* 1 Peter 4:17

There are numerous scriptures describing God's role as Judge (Psalm 75:7, Psalm 50:6, Isaiah 66:16, Hebrews 12:23, James 4:12, Psalm 82:8, Jeremiah 11:20...) with many different attributes. The basic definition of a judge is a public officer authorized to hear and decide cases in a court of law; it is a magistrate charged with the administration of justice[27]. The Greek word for Judge in the parable is kritēs[28]. This word is used about God to mean "a judge who is God of all". This is significant because it suggests that He who is the Judge of His people is at the same time their God[29]. This is an attribute of God as Judge that many of us connect to "judgment day", but not to our daily lives. Nevertheless, it does apply to our daily lives: the way we live, the circumstances we face and essence of who we are. All of it is relevant to God and must be submitted to His judgment, justice and rulership. Taking all of this into consideration, to be consistent and effective in prayer, we must be like the widow repeatedly petitioning our Judge.

The widow was seeking justice, not her own agenda or revenge. This is a mature approach to the Lord when utilizing the court system of Heaven. It speaks to His true lordship in our lives and the rulership He has over us. This must be our heart posture when we approach the Lord in prayer, our Judge in the courts of Heaven. We must seek the righteousness of God, His lawfulness, truth, reason and principles in all matters; and not what our emotions dictate should happen to our adversaries. Honestly, this can be extremely difficult when seeking justice from an adversary as in the case of the widow. In our experience, before entering the courts, our initial step is to seek God and receive His heart about the issue first, and then we proceed to pray His will and justice accurately and effectively.

Therefore, it is important to live a daily life of prayer. We see this demonstrated with the widow as well. It was her consistency and persistence that caused the unjust judge, who had no regard for God or people, to avenge her. In the end, she received the justice she desired. Think about it, if a person without Christ-like characteristics is moved by persistence and consistency, how much more will the God who died for us while we were yet in sin be moved by our consistent, persistent prayer lives? The answer, much more! Jesus says, "*I will avenge them speedily.*" Jesus spent most of His ministry describing the Father's love for us and how much He's willing to do for us (His promises). His promises of us being children of God (Romans 8:15-16, 1 John 3:1), that we are valuable to the Father (Matt. 6:26), He desires to give us good gifts (Matt. 7:9-11), He knows what we need before we ask (Matt. 6:8) and His promises are yes and amen (2 Corinth. 1:19-20) are pretty well-known. Yet, knowledge of His promises does not equal their manifestation in our lives. It is the daily application of these promises that yields manifestation. Therefore, it is imperative for us to be *not only hearers of the Word, but also doers of the Word* (James 1:22-25). The juxtaposition of God and the unjust judge shows how significantly better our position with the Judge is when compared to that of the widow's. I believe that's one of the points that Jesus was trying to make. Knowing that the Father desires to answer us, give us good things and administer His justice on our behalf, serves as encouragement to us all to be more persistent and consistent as the widow was with the judge. It takes a disciplined lifestyle of *prayer without ceasing* (1 Thessalonians 5:17). It requires full surrender to the will of the Lord and his righteousness in our lives. It takes all that and much more to get us in to proper alignment with Heaven.

Even when we don't hear or see the answers we are seeking, we must continue in faith, believing His promise that He hears and will answer. In the parable, Jesus stated the unjust judge did not answer her "*for a while*", yet, during his (the judge's) silence she was not discouraged from praying. And in the same way, we should not lose heart. Jesus ended the parable with this question: will He find faith on the earth upon His return? Faith plays a major role here; our faith not only ensures our perseverance in prayer, but it is the key element in operating in the courts of Heaven. The definition of faith (Hebrews 11:1) tells us that it is both the substance and the evidence we need to continue moving forward despite what we do or do not see. When our hope is in the Lord, (Psalm 33:20-22), we rejoice because of our trust in our Judge who extends to us mercy. For us to walk by faith, our faith must be strong and tangible (2 Corinthians 5:7). So, we must believe and understand that the courts of Heaven are a real place where real decisions are made that affect our lives. Here is an example of how the reality of courts of Heaven have impacted my everyday life:

My family recently celebrated my dad's birthday. I did a court case for the day because I sensed that God wanted to do something very special. In my verdict, I specifically asked that our futures according to the will of the Lord would be discussed along with the next steps of where He was leading each of us. My family and I typically don't have these types of conversations in a group setting. They're often one-on-one conversations. However, for some reason I thought it would be beneficial in celebration of his legacy! As the family gathered, seemingly out of nowhere, one of my sisters began talking about a project she is working on publishing. She asked the group for ideas, went over her plan and we had a great time discussing it. I had no idea my sister was working on a project of that magnitude. And later, I realized that our conversation was a direct result of a petition made in the court case for that day.

A case conducted in a spiritual place, the courtroom of God in Heaven, had a direct result in my family's life that very day! Heaven moved earth to create an opportunity for my sister and I to have a God conversation about her destiny. She was encouraged and in that conversation God poured into her what she needed to fulfill the good works predestined for her. Our conversation was predestined but may not have happened if I didn't engage in the courts of Heaven. Could God have revealed that in prayer without doing a court case? Certainly! There was possibly a plan to delay us from meeting or cause some sort of distraction to prevent the conversation from occurring. Who knows, but God? What I can attest to is my life was directly impacted, in a good way, because of that case.

How did I engage in the courts of Heaven? It was an act of my faith! Faith is a significant factor in building a foundation in the courts; it takes faith to believe. Yes, the faith to believe in what you ask, when the situation applies. However, in this case it's faith to believe THAT THE COURTS ARE A REAL PLACE! Yes, that's right! Say it with me: The courts of Heaven are a real place in Heaven. We can experience the courts without physically dying first (because spiritual death & mortifying our flesh is another subject). It takes faith to believe that this statement is the truth of God and to stand on it by operating in the courts. Since *faith comes by hearing, and hearing by the word of God* (Romans 10:17), we will strengthen our faith in this revelation by studying more examples of it in scripture. Thereby thoroughly examining the nature of these types of supernatural experiences.

SUPERNATURAL SIGHT

There is an abundance of supernatural experiences in the Bible. For the purpose of introducing the revelation of the courts of Heaven, we will be studying two main passages: Daniel 7 and Zechariah 3. Have you ever read any of these stories and thought: where and how are these things taking place? Or do you typically gloss over the reality of these situations?? I am guilty of doing both. As a seer, I see the spiritual realm with both my spiritual and natural eyes. Grasping the reality of this was a difficult journey for me. Not only because it's weird, but also because it serves as an integral part of my identity that stands in direct opposition to the ways of the world. However, having levels of supernatural sight and activity is part of our inheritance as sons of God. The truth is we are supernatural beings having a human experience and it's not the other way around. When we come to the realization that the Old Testament prophets were real men (without a 66-book bible to reference) that had actual encounters with God, the reality of the supernatural and Heaven begins to open up to us like never before. When we start to ask these types of questions, God starts expanding our revelation of His world. For example, where was Daniel taken that enabled him to see everything so vividly? So, begin to ask these types of questions to enable your revelation of the supernatural and Heaven to be expanded.

It is very easy to dismiss the supernatural experiences detailed from cover to cover in the bible as simply figurative or metaphorical. Of course, they have multiple layers of revelation that speak to a multiplicity of situations; however, we cannot discount the reality of those experiences. These things happened to real people: The Red Sea and the Jordan River were split open so that the Israelites could walk through on dry land (Ex. 14:22, Josh. 3:17). The sun legitimately stood still at Joshua's request (Josh. 10:13). Elijah was taken to heaven in a chariot of fire (2 Kings 2:11). Enoch never died (Heb. 11:5). Peter literally walked on water (Matt. 14:29). Lazarus was raised to life after being dead four days (John 11:44). Phillip's physical body translated over 30 miles in a moment's time (Acts 8:39). John walked through a door for the Revelation of Jesus Christ (Rev. 4:1). And the list goes on, but I believe you see my point. How can we get to the "*greater works*" (John 14:12) that we are commissioned to do if we never grasp the reality of these things? We can't. We cannot believe in something without honoring it as reality and we certainly exclude ourselves from the experience by dishonoring it. Jesus displays this principle when He could not do many miracles among the people because they did not honor Him or have faith (Matthew 13:57-59). I encourage you to study each one of these examples with this mindset. Being intentional about expanding our faith, beliefs and actions in the supernatural can be a daunting task, but it is worth it to begin operating in the spiritual world, which is more real than the natural world in which we were born. Everything that exists here (on this earth) is because of what happened in the spiritual world first.

"*By faith we understand that the worlds were framed by the word of God, so that the things, which are seen, were not made of things, which are visible.*"
Hebrews 11:3

"*While we look not at the things which are seen, but at the things which are not seen: for the things which are seen are temporal; but the things which are not seen are eternal.*" 2 Corinthians 4:18

2nd Corinthians instructs us to LOOK at the things that are not seen, to look at the invisible. This implies that things that are deemed invisible can somehow be seen; however, we are not naturally inclined to see them. There are a few more scripture references that discuss the invisible. The Greek word translated as invisible "aoratos" literally means unseen[5]. The word unseen has a connotation of something that is capable of being seen, but is hidden or concealed. It is only used a few times in scripture, each of which gives clarity on how we should engage with the invisible.

"*By faith he left Egypt, not fearing the king's anger; he persevered because he saw him who is invisible.*" Hebrews 11:27

"*For the invisible things of him from the creation of the world are clearly seen, being understood by the things that are made, even his eternal power and Godhead; so that they are without excuse.*" Romans 1:20

These scriptures not only support the idea that invisible things can be seen… they prove it! Moses persevered BECAUSE he saw Him who is invisible. That is a significant statement for many reasons, but we should be encouraged that we, too, can see the invisible. This level of sight in the supernatural enabled Moses to persevere. The same can be true for us because God is not a respecter of persons (Romans 2:11). Along with this, Paul tells us that the invisible things of God are clearly seen. Wow! I read this scripture many times, before that revelation really hit me: the invisible things are clearly seen.

I understand that this may seem outlandish to some because it is far from our normal realm of thinking. And that's okay! The point here is to bridge the gap between a) what is normal/natural for us and b) the supernatural world of the God we serve. We must stretch our faith and belief systems to apprehend these biblical truths as a crucial step for our growth and maturity. It is essential that we first bridge the gaps within ourselves in order to be the bridge that brings heaven into earth. This is another reason why we need to discipline ourselves to live a consecrated lifestyle and walk in the Spirit. These are non-negotiable when operating in the supernatural, Heavenly realm. This daily life of being led by the Spirit is the lifestyle of the Sons of God, according to Romans 8:13-17:

"*For if ye live after the flesh, ye shall die: but if ye through the Spirit do mortify the deeds of the body, ye shall live* [14] *For as many as are led by the Spirit of God, they are the sons of God.* [15] *For ye have not received the spirit of bondage again to fear; but ye have received the Spirit of adoption, whereby we cry, Abba, Father.* [16] *The Spirit itself bears witness with our spirit, that we are the children of God:* [17] *And if children, then heirs; heirs of God, and joint-heirs with Christ; if so be that we suffer with him, that we may be also glorified together.*"

God has given us the power to achieve this lifestyle:

"*But as many as received him, to them gave he power to become the sons of God, even to them that believe on his name:* [13] *Which were born, not of blood, nor of the will of the flesh, nor of the will of man, but of God.*" John 1:12-13

So, as with anything in our walk with Christ, it is not up to us to accomplish this transformation. We are not capable of accomplishing such a feat on our own. However, it is essential that we partner with God by walking in the Spirit daily to open ourselves up to the revelation and transformational power He desires to bring into our lives.

"[9] *But as it is written: 'Eye has not seen, nor ear heard, Nor have entered into the heart of man the things which God has prepared for those who love Him.'* [10] *But God has revealed them to us through His Spirit. For the Spirit searches all things, yes, the deep things of God.* [11] *For what man knows the things of a man except the spirit of the man, which is in him? Even so no one knows the things of God except the Spirit of God.* [12] *Now we have received, not the spirit of the world, but the Spirit who is from God, that we might know the things that have been freely given to us by God."* 1 Corinthians 2:9-12

For the passages we will be examining, there are key phrases used in the accounts of these supernatural experiences such as: "*I looked*", "*he shewed*", and "*I beheld*". Taking a deeper look at these key phrases will help us to better grasp the context of each experience.

In Daniel 7:9-12, Daniel uses the phrase "I beheld…" The Hebrew word for beheld is "châzâh", which means to see, behold, to gaze upon or to perceive[31]. In Zechariah 3:1-7, Zechariah says "*he shewed me…"* prior to describing what he saw. The Hebrew word here for shewed is "râ'âh", which means to see, observe, perceive, get acquainted with or examine[32]. The Hebrew context of using these words connotes seeing with one's natural eyes. They are also used in the sense of seeing only what is obvious; this holds much significance as it gives new weight to the type of supernatural sight these men had and the reality of their experiences with the Lord. These experiences were not a result of daydreams or vain imaginations happening in their minds. Am I saying if you were sitting beside them during these moments you would have the same experiences? No, what I am saying is these men grew to a place in God to see supernaturally what was happening in the spirit realm with their natural eyes. It became obvious to them.

Although this is not one of our specific examples of study for the courts, John's experience in the Revelation of Jesus Christ parallels Daniel's description of the courts. It is also a great New Testament example of supernatural sight and our ability to participate in heavenly activity while living on earth. As John starts to describe his interactions in Revelation 4, he is on the island of Patmos, alive and well, discussing what he saw and heard.

"*After this I looked, and, behold, a door was opened in heaven: and the first voice which I heard was as it were of a trumpet talking with me; which said, Come up hither, and I will show thee things which must be hereafter. And immediately I was in the spirit: and, behold, a throne was set in heaven, and one sat on the throne."* Revelation 4:1-2

Again, note the words looked and behold are used to describe what took place. In Greek, these words are "eídō", which means to see, to know by perception, look, perceive, behold, or be aware; and "idou", which means to see, calling attention to what may be seen or heard or mentally apprehended[33]. They are used to express merely mechanical, passive or casual vision. So John sees a door in Heaven AND THEN is in the Spirit experiencing all of these things. He gives great detail about activity that is taking place around the throne of God. This is a place that we as children of God are invited to come boldly in Hebrews 4:16. It is a scripture that is very well known and often quoted, but do we grasp the reality of the access we have to the King? For most of us, the answer is no, we don't. Nevertheless, it is a privilege and right that we were granted access to these holy places by the death, burial and resurrection of Jesus Christ according to Hebrews 10:19-22. And not just figuratively either:

"*But God, who is rich in mercy, for his great love wherewith he loved us, [5]Even when we were dead in sins, hath quickened us together with Christ, (by grace ye are saved;) [6]And hath raised us up together, and made us sit together in heavenly places in Christ Jesus.*" Ephesians 2:4-6

Many of us quickly claim the fact that we are seated in Heavenly places (and we are!), having little to no understanding of what this looks like in our daily lives. I know I was personally guilty of this. Seats represent rulership and authority. Which begs the question: How are you called to rule and reign with Jesus in your personal life? The ability to fill in the blanks comes from diligence in walking in the Spirit and living a supernatural life. If nothing else, we should recognize that levels of supernatural sight and activity are not only attainable, but should be a norm for EVERY believer.

DANIEL'S VISION OF A COURT CASE

You may be thinking, "Okay, I think I get it, but you're going to have to show me where these courts are actually seen in scripture." My pleasure! One of our favorite passages of scripture about the courts of Heaven is found in Daniel 7. This chapter begins with a description of 4 great beasts coming out of the sea. The beasts represented 4 great kingdoms that would arise and fall over the course of time.

Next, Daniel shares with us a real live court proceeding he witnessed in Heaven. Don't believe me, just watch! That verse reads:

> [9]*I kept looking, Until thrones were set up, and the Ancient of Days took His seat; His vesture was like white snow, and the hair of His head like pure wool. His throne was ablaze with flames, its wheels were a burning fire.*
> [10] *"A river of fire was flowing And coming out from before Him; Thousands upon thousands were attending Him, and myriads upon myriads were standing before Him; The court sat, And the books were opened.* [11] *Then I kept looking because of the sound of the boastful words which the horn was speaking; I kept looking until the beast was slain, and its body was destroyed and given to the burning fire.*

[12] As for the rest of the beasts, their dominion was taken away, but an extension of life was granted to them for an appointed period of time. Daniel 7:9-12

This scripture is a clear picture of a court case happening in real time! God, the Ancient of Days, was seated, and thousands were present serving His interests. The court sat and the books were opened. The horn spoke, making its case in prideful boasts. Then, the gavel landed, judgment was rendered, and the beast was slain. Next, God passed a verdict against the other beasts, the other kingdoms that rose out of the sea. From this chapter, we see that God called the kings before Him to render judgment against them.

But the court proceeding did not end there. In this same chapter, in verses 23 through 27, Daniel is speaking with a person in Heaven who explains the court proceeding he was witnessing. He explained that the fourth beast was a fourth kingdom different than the previous three and it would devour the earth and subdue three other kings. The ruler of the fourth kingdom would wage war against believers and blaspheme the Most High. For a moment he would prevail, but the court would sit for judgment, and this evil one's dominion would be removed and destroyed. And his dominion of all the kingdoms of the earth would be given to the saints of the Most High God.

This scripture was a real proceeding in Heaven that is yet unfolding in the earth today. In fact, as you are reading this book you are fruit of this case in Heaven. If you are a child of God, you are a saint of the Most High and will inherit Kingdoms, to establish the dominion of Heaven. Reading this book is preparing you for that day. From this scripture, we see the components of a court case. There is a judge, there are ones being judged, there are people standing as witnesses of the case, a verdict is rendered and God's will prevailed!

ZECHARIAH'S EXPERIENCE IN THE COURTS

Now, let's look at a passage of scripture that describes a courtroom interaction, Zechariah 3:1-7. As you read, keep in mind what we learned about these supernatural experiences with God and extend your faith to believe. This was a real event that he and Joshua experienced in the Spirit together.

"*Then he showed me Joshua the high priest standing before the Angel of the Lord, and Satan standing at his right hand to oppose him.* [2] *And the Lord said to Satan, "The Lord rebuke you, Satan! The Lord who has chosen Jerusalem rebuke you! Is this not a brand plucked from the fire?"* [3] *Now Joshua was clothed with filthy garments, and was standing before the Angel.* [4] *Then He answered and spoke to those who stood before Him, saying, "Take away the filthy garments from him." And to him He said, "See, I have removed your iniquity from you, and I will clothe you with rich robes."* [5] *And I said, "Let them put a clean turban on his head." So they put a clean turban on his head, and they put the clothes on him. And the Angel of the Lord stood by.* [6] *Then the Angel of the Lord admonished Joshua, saying,* [7] *"Thus says the Lord of hosts: 'If you will walk in My ways,*
And if you will keep My command,
Then you shall also judge My house,
And likewise have charge of My courts;
I will give you places to walk
Among these who stand here."

Whoa! This passage displays a complete discourse in the courts play-by-play:

1. Satan accuses Joshua.
2. God rebukes satan because of the call on Joshua's life (to rebuild Jerusalem).
3. Joshua was dirty.
4. God commanded his dirty garments to be removed and promised to give him clean ones.
5. The angels remove his dirty clothes.

6. The prophet, Zechariah, commands clean garments to be put on him.
7. They put clean garments on him.
8. God gave him authority in the courts of Heaven to render judgments and set things in order.

There are a lot of details going on in the above proceedings. The enemy is opposing Joshua through accusations; a process he constantly uses to oppose the body of Christ (Rev. 12:10), which we will get more into later. Without Joshua saying a word, or even attempting to make his own case, God rebukes satan. He uses the call on Joshua's life to justify (as evidence against the rebuke); thereby the accusations of satan could not stand because this is His chosen vessel for the work in Jerusalem. This demonstrates how important the destiny and scroll of our lives are in thwarting satan's attempts to derail God's will for our lives. Joshua had a very specific, weighty call on his life and knowing that proved powerfully in His defense.

Let's dissect this further: It says Joshua was "*clothed with filthy garments*"; the filthy garments represented his iniquity. So, God rebuked satan on behalf of Joshua even while he was yet in iniquity (still dirty), just like Jesus died for all of us while we were yet in sin (Romans 5:8). This is a substantial principle of the Lord we need to understand as His children. God does not require that we are clean, perfect, have it all together, or without sin to come to Him. In fact, it's the direct opposite, we need to come to God to become clean, to be perfected, get it all together and have our sin dealt with completely. This passage displays this principle wonderfully. This doesn't negate the need for us to speak for ourselves in court; it's symbolic of what God is willing to do before we even say a word.

Did you notice from the passage everyone that came to testify on behalf of Joshua? Not only was the command and promise of the Lord for Joshua to be cleaned, there was also the participation of the angels and the prophet to carry it out at the word of the Lord. The angels remove his filth and the prophet instructs them to place clean garments on him, as the Lord had promised. Therefore, along with the word of the Lord, angelic participation and prophetic insight are necessary for us to receive the fullness of freedom and promises that God has for us. All of these elements work together. Our cleanliness and holiness is essential to God's will being done in our lives; without this dynamic duo the enemy can prevent us from accessing and manifesting according to our books in Heaven. Yet, this is a step-by-step process:

satan Rebuked → Joshua Cleansed & Clothed → New Authority Given

After the accusations were nullified and Joshua was redeemed, God restored the authority of the call on his life. If Joshua remained in the will of God, he had the authority to judge His house, the charge of His courts and a place among those ruling in Heaven. Because of this court process, Joshua can render judgments and set things in order for Jerusalem as he was chosen to do. Now we can clearly see that the courts of Heaven are the place to resolve the legalities in our lives (held up with accusations of satan & iniquity) and receive new garments. It is the place where our [God-imputed] holiness pleads our case before God and we receive official authority to execute God's judgment in the earth.

ADDRESSING ACCUSATIONS TO SEE TRANSFORMATION

One question we ask as Believers in Christ is "why, after praying about a matter for years, DO we NOT see any results?" It doesn't make sense. We pray, we fast, we decree, and NOTHING changes! We confess scriptures and are praying in accordance with God's will, and still we see no positive movement in our lives. We go through a process of repentance, repenting of everything we can think of and yet no progress day after day, month after month, and year after year, we face the same issues. Issues that, if not dealt with, we will cause us to develop coping mechanisms to hide, deflect or accept as part of who we are. Understand, it's not a part of who you are that's a LIE from the pit of hell! From the perspective of the courts of Heaven, the primary reasons we experience this frustrating blockade is simply due to accusations in our lives and in the lives of our ancestors preventing the will of God from fully being accomplished in our lives.

What is an accusation? It is a charge of wrongdoing.[34] Due a lack of revelation of Heaven's court system, we miss the "due process" of Heaven necessary to enforce the work Jesus completed at the cross. Completing this due process is needful to see permanent advancement in our lives. What do I mean by this? Imagine this: you see a house for sale in your area and you are certain God said, "this house is for you, child." Can you simply move into the house right then? Could you pack up and move in the next day? If tried, you would face some opposition. Why? Even though God ordained that house to be yours, there are legal due processes that you must complete to take possession of that home. The moment God said the house was yours, it legally belonged to someone else. Therefore, there are key steps you must take to obtain legal ownership and rights to that property.

Yes, it is a possibility that we are ignorant as to what steps or processes are needed, however, our ignorance doesn't deny the fact that the legalities exist. One could say, "I didn't know there was a process for taking possession of the home, and God said it's mine!" Though this is true, it doesn't change the fact that there is still a process set in place to purchase a home and that process cannot be bypassed! It can be expedited, made easier, and you can experience crazy favor. But there are still basic tenets of law that must be followed for the transaction to happen legally.

So, let's take this scenario a bit further, what if you illegally took possession of the home. How would one fair? Its current owner has the right to take legal action against you, right? Because you attempted to occupy something that rightfully belongs to someone else. When we commit sins, iniquities and transgressions, we give the enemy legal recourse against us. As we trespass against the will of God, we operate in darkness, the realm where satan rules.

But, rest assured we have an advocate in Jesus because we are found in Jesus. He paid the ultimate price for every accusation against us. Through Heaven's court system and our covenant with Jesus as our Messiah, we invoke the blood of Jesus as a witness (for our forgiven sins) and our accusations are nullified through his blood.

PLEADING THE BLOOD OF JESUS

If you have been in certain denominations, such as Charismatic or Pentecostal, for any period of time, the phrase "I plead the blood of Jesus…" is quite familiar to you. If not, as a believer, you know that Jesus' blood paid the full price for our lives, setting us free from the penalty of death that our sin required. To plead is to present and argue for a position, cause or case, especially in a court or other public context[35]. While this specific phrasing isn't found in scripture, its concept is biblical. Another way to describe it would be to appropriate the blood of Jesus – to set apart, authorize, or legislate it for some specific purpose or use[36]. In this case, it would be for reconciliation in our individual lives.

"*For the life of the flesh is in the blood, and I have given it to you upon the altar to make atonement for your souls; for it is the blood that makes atonement for the soul.*" Leviticus 17:11

The process of atonement the Old Testament priests carried out was a legal transaction. Atonement is the satisfaction or reparation for a wrong or injury; to make amends, reconciliation or agreement[37]. Blood (death) was the requirement to pay the debt of sin. When the priests shed the blood of animals, the mercy of God was released and the sins of the nation were absolved for one year. The shedding of Jesus' blood as He was sacrificed on the cross was the ultimate fulfillment of this process for us.

Nonetheless, we don't always see the fullness of this transaction in our lives. People live for Christ year after year, decade after decade without seeing these promises manifested in their lives. How can this be? It is because we fail to appropriate (authorize, legislate) everything the shedding of His blood did for our lives. Jesus died for the world to be saved (John 3:16-17); yet many in the world still need salvation. The beating that He endured gave us access to healing (Isaiah 53:5); however, many (believers) are yet plagued by disease. This doesn't mean His death, burial and resurrection wasn't sufficient or has lost its power! It is however, an indication that we have not applied all of the benefits of His blood to our lives. This is why accepting Jesus as our Lord and Savior is a continual process; to walk out each step of salvation in our own personal lives (Philippians 2:12) and see the fullness of what He did on the cross manifest in our lives.

According to Webster, to appropriate something is to take exclusive possession of it, to set apart for or to assign to a particular purpose/use[38]. In this case, we are discussing the necessity of believers taking the exclusive possession of the Blood of Jesus and applying it to the issues at work in our personal lives. Again, we are absolutely not redoing the work of the cross! Jesus fully completed that work; it is finished! (Colossians 1:19-22, Ephesians 1:7). We are referring to applying and enforcing the power of the Blood until our lives match that which is written in the scriptures, the true ministry of reconciliation.

"[14] *For Christ's love compels us, because we are convinced that one died for all, and therefore all died.* [15] *And he died for all, that those who live should no longer live for themselves but for him who died for them and was raised again.* [16] *So from now on we regard no one from a worldly point of view. Though we once regarded Christ in this way, we do so no longer.* [17] *Therefore, if anyone is in Christ, the new creation has come: The old has gone, the new is here!* [18] *All this is from God, who reconciled us to himself through Christ and gave us the ministry of reconciliation:* [19] *that God was reconciling the world to himself in Christ, not counting people's sins against them. And he has committed to us the message of reconciliation.* [20] *We are therefore Christ's ambassadors, as though God were making his appeal through us. We implore you on Christ's behalf: Be reconciled to God. [21] God made him who had no sin to be sin for us, so that in him we might become the righteousness of God."* 2 Corinthians 5:14-21

Here, Paul is talking to the Corinthians, which means he is dealing with believers, and not unbelievers (not people without salvation). Yet, he is imploring them to "*Be Reconciled to God*". Imploring is similar to beseeching; it is an earnest plea, insistence and urgently asking for something to happen[39]. By Paul making this statement it implies that there is a **process** to our reconciliation. Though accepting Christ and receiving salvation immediately grant us access to all the promises of God, all the benefits of salvation do not manifest immediately. There is still work required on our end. Paul would not make such a passionate plea "*on Christ's behalf*" if there wasn't a need for the Corinthian church to be reconciled. He recognized there was a gap, a disconnection that must be bridged. Appropriating the Blood of Jesus is the key in bridging the gap. So, how do we apply this in our individual lives? Where do we plead the blood of Jesus? This happens in the courts of Heaven. In this very real place, we address legalities and receive authority from God. When we go through the process of repenting for our sins, transgressions, and iniquities, – thereby answering the accuser – we can appropriate Jesus' blood to our lives and our bloodlines.

"[10] *Then I heard a loud voice saying in heaven, "Now salvation, and strength, and the kingdom of our God, and the power of His Christ have come, for the accuser of our brethren, who accused them before our God day and night, has been cast down. [11] And they overcame him by the blood of the Lamb and by the word of their testimony, and they did not love their lives to the death."*

Revelation 12:10-11

The accuser of the brethren – our enemy, satan – is overcome by the Blood of Jesus. By testifying and applying the Blood to our lives, satan is silenced and his accusations must cease. At this point, we must acknowledge more of the supernatural characteristics of blood: mainly, the fact that it speaks and has a voice. This is not only a characteristic of Jesus' blood; it is a superiority of blood period. The first time we see this is with Cain and Abel.

"8 Now Cain talked with Abel his brother; and it came to pass, when they were in the field,
that Cain rose up against Abel his brother and killed him. 9 Then the Lord said to Cain,
'Where is Abel your brother?' He said, 'I do not know. Am I my brother's keeper?' 10 And He
said, 'What have you done? The voice of your brother's blood cries out to Me from the
ground. 11 So now you are cursed from the earth, which has opened its mouth to receive
your brother's blood from your hand. 12 When you till the ground, it shall no longer yield its
strength to you. A fugitive and a vagabond you shall be on the earth." Genesis 4:8-12

The Lord says the voice of Abel's blood "*cried out to Him from the ground*". Again, this is not figurative, metaphoric or an embodiment. Abel's blood spoke to God and testified of his murder. This testimony caused God to curse Cain for the act he committed against his brother. This however, is not the only instance of blood speaking in the bible.

"... and to the blood of sprinkling that speaks better things that that of Abel."
Hebrews 12:24

"9 When He opened the fifth seal, I saw under the altar the souls of those who had been
slain for the word of God and for the testimony which they held. 10 And they cried with a
loud voice, saying, "How long, O Lord, holy and true, until You judge and avenge our blood
on those who dwell on the earth?" 11 Then a white robe was given to each of them; and it
was said to them that they should rest a little while longer, until both the number of their fellow servants and their brethren, who would be killed as they were, was completed."
Revelation 6:9-11

These two scriptures discuss the Blood of Jesus and the blood of the martyrs, respectively, and show evidence of blood testifying or speaking. Those killed for the cause of the Kingdom are under the throne, and their blood continually cries out for justice. Their upmost desire is that the purpose for which their lives were sacrificed be fulfilled in the earth. Jesus' blood, of course, has the greatest and most prevailing voice and it is constantly crying out for our complete salvation and restoration. We must learn to come into agreement with the testimony of His blood; to do so, we must first know what His blood is saying about us. Here is a list of many of the ways Jesus' blood speaks for us.

21 Ways the Blood of Jesus Testifies on our Behalf

1. Satisfies our transgressions & iniquities and gives us peace. (Isaiah 53:5)
2. We can commune with Him by the New Covenant. (Luke 22:20)
3. It gives us life. (John 6:53)
4. It purchased the Church. (Acts 20:28)
5. We are justified and saved from wrath. (Romans 5:9)
6. We can become the righteousness of God. (2 Corinthians 5:21)
7. Christ lives in us. (Galatians 2:20)
8. We are redeemed from the curse of the law. (Galatians 3:13)
9. We have freedom and liberty. (Galatians 5:1)
10. We have access to the covenant of promise and are near to Him. (Ephesians 2:12-13)
11. It ministers reconciliation to us. (Colossians 1:19-22)
12. We have power over principalities and powers of darkness. (Colossians 2:15)
13. Our consciences are cleansed from dead works. (Hebrews 9:14)
14. It paid the debt of sin. (Hebrews 9:28)
15. We can boldly enter the Holiest of Holies. (Hebrews 10:19-22)
16. We are sanctified. (Hebrews 13:12)
17. Our redemption is incorruptible. (1 Peter 1:18-19)

18. We are healed and can live in righteousness. (1 Peter 2:24)
19. It cleanses us. (1John 1:7)
20. We are kings and priests. (Revelation 1:5)
21. It causes us to be overcomers. (Revelation 12:11)

Of course, this list is not exhaustive, but it provides a wonderful foundation in understanding the testimony of the Blood of Jesus. Now that we know specifically what Jesus' blood established for us, we can agree with it and appropriate it to our lives. Our agreement gives us access to its power of forgiveness and redemption (Ephesians 1:7). His blood is applied for our justification.

Agreement is a powerful tool that brings us into unity with God and His ordained will for our lives. This is a key method in prayer: reminding God of His word and basing our requests on that. It's the agreement principle at work once again! As stated before, God is one with His word (John 1:1), which is already settled in Heaven (Psalm 119:89). It is His mandate to use us to pray for things to be on earth as they are in Heaven (Matthew 6:10). This is how we appropriate His blood and request verdicts in the courts. Using the courts we begin to establish Kingdom influence, reign and dominion in the earth. Here's the clincher, the court is rigged in our favor! As we come requesting God's will we can be confident in this very thing that the price was paid in full. However, we must show up to court to appropriate the blood that has already been shed for us. The process of activating the finished work of the cross is carried out in the courts of Heaven.

As His confessions become our confessions, the weight of His glory will back His word and as Isaiah 55:11 states *His word will not return to Him void.* It is on this foundation (agreement with the word of God) that we operate in the courts of Heaven and see verdicts rendered on our behalf. We receive clarity when we come into a full revelation of what the promises of God, in addition to His death, burial and resurrection, accomplished for us. Then we can see the areas of our lives that are out of alignment with His will. As these areas are revealed, we address them by bringing correction/alignment through the word of God and applying His blood. The application of His blood activates what Jesus paid a price for, the remission of our sins.

We adjudicate in the courts by saying "oh, yes", agreeing with the accusations against our bloodline and ourselves. We incorporate the blood of Jesus to testify and the accusations are pardoned through His sacrifice. And guess what? Even though the accusation was valid it can no longer stand because of the blood of Jesus! What a price He paid for us ALL! Jesus' blood will not stop testifying until all that it accomplished on the cross is legally appropriated, manifested and established in the earth. Dominion is impossible without Kingdom governmental rulership and the establishment of its laws and culture. This is our role as the church, the ecclēsia, of God: using our authority to get judgments rendered and set things in order in the earth according to God's Kingdom – as He said to Joshua.

---

[26] Dictionary Online, http://www.dictionary.com/browse/petition

[27] Dictionary Online, http://www.dictionary.com/browse/judge

[28] Strong LL.D., S.T.D., James. The New Strong's Expanded Exhaustive Concordance of The Bible, G2923, page 145

[29] Vine, W.E., Unger, Merrill F., White Jr., William. Vine's Complete Expository Dictionary of Old & New Testament Words, page 336

[30] Strong, LL. D., S.T.D., James. The New Strong's Expanded Exhaustive Concordance of the Bible, G517, page 31

[31] Strong, James. The New Strong's Expanded Exhaustive Concordance of the Bible, H2370, page 83

[32] Strong, James. The New Strong's Expanded Exhaustive Concordance of the Bible, H7200, page 253

[33] Strong, James. The New Strong's Expanded Exhaustive Concordance of the Bible, G1492, G2400, Pages 76, 119

[34] https://www.merriam-webster.com/dictionary/accusation

[35] Oxford Dictionary Online, https://en.oxforddictionaries.com/definition/plead

[36] Dictionary Online, http://www.dictionary.com/browse/appropriate

[37] Merriam-Webster Online, https://www.merriam-webster.com/dictionary/atonement

[38] Merriam-Webster Online, https://www.merriam-webster.com/dictionary/appropriate

[39] Dictionary online, http://www.dictionary.com/browse/beseech

CHAPTER 6 REVIEW QUESTIONS

1. What aspect of the nature of God is it important to understand in order to operate in the government of Heaven?
2. What is the basic definition of prayer? Define this word.
3. Where does Jesus place prayer? What happens in this example?
4. Why did Moses persevere?
5. What are 3 key elements that worked together for Joshua's redemption? How so?
6. Where do we go to bring our petitions and address accusations brought against us in the spiritual realm?
7. Why have we not seen lasting change after applying all of the principles of prayer that we've learned throughout our lives?
8. Name 5 ways the Blood of Jesus testifies on our behalf.

Chapter 7: The Role of The Accuser

When we operate in the courts of Heaven we are addressing the accusations that keep us in bondage. Unaddressed accusations can prevent us from living out the fullness of the destiny God has for us.

Do understand, accusations do not arbitrarily show up out of thin air. Yes, God knows all things, but He is not our accuser in court. The one who is called the accuser of the brethren, satan, presents accusations against us constantly. It is satan's accusation that we address in the courts, not any accusations brought against us by God. We are not exalting satan by any means. However, he has a role in the government of heaven just as we do. In fact, Proverbs 16:4-5 says, *"[4] The Lord has made everything for its own purpose, Even the wicked for the day of evil. [5] Everyone who is proud in heart is an abomination to the Lord; Assuredly, he will not be unpunished."*

Satan's wickedness serves a purpose: to draw the line of distinction between what clearly is and is not of God. As the Proverbs states, satan's wickedness *will not go unpunished.* However, we must be aware of the enemy's devices, schemes and tactics. Through our awareness, we can understand his accusations against us, as well as the traps, bondages and prisons set in our lives to keep us bound in darkness and unable to live out our destinies.

Yes, we were translated to the Kingdom of light, but the reality of this truth of being translated to this new kingdom is received through revelation. In this chapter, we will learn who our accuser is, what he accuses of and how we can address his accusations. When we settle the accusations, they can no longer keep us from our God and the good life He has for us.

DISOBEDIENCE AND REBELLION: FOUNDATIONS OF INIQUITY

In her book, *Iniquity - The Major Hindrance to Seeing God's Glory Manifested*, Anna Mendez Ferrell describes iniquity as the body of sin, the spiritual inheritance of evil transmitted through our DNA at conception.[40] Iniquity is the propensity towards living in an ungodly way with regard to our thoughts, intents, actions and habits. Iniquity entered the world when Adam and Eve chose to disobey God in the Garden of Eden and eat from the tree of the knowledge of good and evil. First, they listened to the voice of satan, the seducer, and then believed him. They chose to believe the voice of one other than their Creator. In doing so, they disobeyed God and rebelled against His command. In this moment of disobedience, the entire history of mankind was changed. Rather than our only frame of reference for existence being communion with God, it became our carnal nature. At this moment, the conflict between living according to the nature of God and carnality began as well.

The first Adam's choice to disobey God became a pattern for living for all mankind. It opened our world up to the influence of evil and as time went on man gave himself more and more to its carnal nature, and iniquity took a firmer root. From this story of the fall of man in the Garden of Eden, we see that iniquity was birthed through disobedience to God and rebellion against His desired way of communion with us.

INIQUITY VERSUS SIN VERSUS TRANSGRESSIONS

In Christendom, we often use iniquity, sin and transgression interchangeably to refer to the overall act of disobedience to God. However, each of these words refers to three different conditions of the fallen nature.

In Psalm 51, David states:

[1]Be gracious to me, O God, according to Your loving-kindness; according to the greatness of Your compassion blot out my transgressions. [2] Wash me thoroughly from my iniquity, and cleanse me from my sin. [3]For I know my transgressions, and my sin is ever before me.

The Strong's concordance shows that iniquity in this scripture is the Hebrew word "`avon". This word is defined as perversity (moral evil), fault, mischief and punishment for sin.[41] The root word for `avon is "`avah", which means to crook, to do amiss, bow down, make crooked, commit iniquity, pervert, (do) perverse(-ly), trouble, turn, do wickedly, or to do wrong.[42] The definition of iniquity is the seed and wicked DNA that is passed down in the bloodline. Iniquity sets the whole pattern of ungodliness.

Example of Iniquity: (Ungodly DNA in the bloodline)

1. **Ungodly generational patterns**: the inheritance of evil that is transmitted that corrupts the soul. This corruption carries an innate desire or proclivity to do wrong from generation to generation. This is the reason that a son of an alcoholic inherits an insatiable desire to drink.[43]

Iniquity is the root of the sins and transgressions we commit, however, iniquity itself is caused by the repeated occurrence of transgressions and sin. Let's examine this deeper.

The root word of transgression in the Old Testament is "pasha`".[44] This word means, "to revolt, rebel, to breakaway and to offend." When we transgress the way of God, we rebel against Him. We are revolting against His will, thereby leaving ourselves open to the accusations and the bondage of satan. Therefore, a transgression is a violation of the law; an offense or infringement. Transgressions are willful acts of disobedience and infractions against God.

Example of Transgression (Ungodly actions)

1. Harm to others and ourselves: Fighting, cursing backstabbing, gossiping, complaining, etc.

2. **Word curses we speak/Word curses spoken over us**:
"Death and life are in the power of the tongue…" Proverbs 18:21

Transgression produces a heart posture of defiance. Thereby, we transgress the way of God. When we remain in this sinful state and do not turn from our acts of sin and transgressions to allow God to purify us, our way becomes perverted and more iniquity is birthed. Repeated transgressions for which we do not repent cause us to live a life of sin. The root word for sin in Hebrew is "chata'".[45] "Chata'" means to miss, forefeit, lack and lead astray. When we sin, we "miss the mark" and fall short of the glory of God, which leads us astray from the path of God. Sin is the perverted desire of the heart. It is the thought and intent against the laws of God. Matthew 5:28 says this,

"But I say unto you, that whosoever looketh on a woman to lust after her hath committed adultery with her already in his heart."

Jesus talks of how when you simply lust after a person, you have committed adultery. Our ungodly motives are still counted as sin because it was purposed in the heart to transgress God's will; though the physical act of the adultery was not committed. The thoughts and intents of our heart are powerful and they are the guiding force behind why we do what we do.

The act of going astray through disobedience leads to a state of sinfulness; faulty living that leads to death and destruction because we are disconnected from the source of light and life, God Himself. In this state of sinfulness, we are subject to the enemy's schemes and our thoughts become perverted because we are not living in the way of life, the way of God. Therefore, when the accuser stands against us before God in court, he accuses us of our transgressions (actions), our motives and thoughts (sins), and our iniquities (perversions) in our bloodline.

ACCUSER OF THE BRETHREN

One name for satan is the accuser of the brethren. This name was used to describe him in Revelation 12. Here, Michael the angel and his team fought against satan and his team in Heaven. Michael and the holy angels of God overpowered satan and the evil angels and they were cast down to the earth. Then in Revelation 12:10, the scripture says, *"Now the salvation, and the power, and the kingdom of our God and the authority of His Christ have come, for the accuser of our brethren has been thrown down, he who accuses them before our God day and night."*

Because this book is not a study of end-time theology, we will not attempt to interpret the meaning of this scripture. It is a suggested study in your free time. The point to note and learn from this verse is satan accuses us day and night, night and day. 1 Peter 5:8 further tells us, *"Be of sober spirit, be on the alert. Your adversary, the devil, prowls around like a roaring lion, seeking someone to devour."*

When we refer to an accuser, we are not just speaking of a person who accuses you of doing something. We are referring to the devil that has made it his business to see the demise of humanity. He testifies of the darkness in and committed by man that prevents God's will from being accomplished in our lives.

WHO THE ACCUSER IS NOT

As stated previously, when we refer to the accuser, we are speaking in the context of the courts of Heaven. This is very key! There are people who accuse us of things, some true and some untrue. However, for the purposes of this book, we are not speaking of people. From the scriptures, it is clear, that the devil, satan, is our accuser in the government of God. It's essential to know that your accuser is not:

1. Your ex
2. Your estranged sibling
3. Your demanding boss
4. That person who honked at you on the road
5. The people who teased and bullied you
6. The co-workers who gossip about you
7. Your grieving friend
8. Your distant spouse
9. Your rebellious child

[10]Are these relationships difficult sometimes? Yes! Do these people accuse you? Yes! However, there is one very important thing you must remember: *"Finally, be strong in the Lord and in the strength of His might. [11] Put on the full armor of God, so that you will be able to stand firm against the schemes of the devil. [12] For our struggle is not against flesh and blood, but against the rulers, against the powers, against the world forces of this darkness, against the spiritual forces of wickedness in the heavenly places. [13] Therefore, take up the full armor of God, so that you will be able to resist in the evil day, and having done everything, to stand firm,"* Ephesians 6:11-13 (Selah, pause and calmly let that sink in).

A CURSE WITHOUT CAUSE CANNOT LAND

It's impossible for satan to lie before God. He is not permitted to do so. Isn't that wonderful news!? God will not come into agreement with satan's lies and deceit. He can only operate according to the law of God.

Psalm 89:14 tells us, "*Righteousness and justice are the foundation of Your throne; Loving-kindness and truth go before You.*" God is just and can only do what is right. With that said, when we are accused (by satan) and there's evidence of a curse at work: It is proof the accusation is legitimate. Proverbs 26:2 states, *"Like a sparrow in its flitting, like a swallow in its flying, so a curse without cause does not alight."* This scripture gives new meaning to the maxim, "everything happens for a reason".

Ephesians 2:1-3 gives a clear picture of what the untransformed life looks like.

> [1]*And you were dead in your trespasses and sins,* [2] *in which you formerly walked according to the course of this world, according to the prince of the power of the air, of the spirit that is now working in the sons of disobedience.* [3] *Among them we too all formerly lived in the lusts of our flesh, indulging the desires of the flesh and of the mind, and were by nature children of wrath, even as the rest.*

Prior to salvation, we were exactly as this scripture states, children of wrath, living according to our sinful nature and in complete enmity with God. Once we believe in Jesus as our Messiah and are birthed into the family of God, we are made new beings. When Jesus redeems us, there is still a process to experiencing the full transformation His death and resurrection accomplished for us.

As we learned in Chapter 6, the blood of Jesus is necessary because His blood answers the accusations brought against us by Satan. But appropriating the blood of Jesus is an action; something one must do proactively.

Satan accuse us of the sins, iniquities and transgressions we (and those in our bloodline) have committed. Sins, iniquities and transgressions are offenses that are birthed from rebellion and against God. It's the law of sowing and reaping in play. If we live according to the law of sin and death, we will reap the fruit thereof. If we sow sin, we reap its punishment. If we sow transgression, we reap rebellion and discord. In our lack of communion with God and continued disobedience against following His way for our lives, we lose the protection of being found in His will. With the loss of His protection, we are opened to being influenced by the kingdom of darkness.

Every accusation brought against you applies to you or to someone in your ancestry. When our ancestors do not deal with iniquities, the record of their offenses pass on to us as their children. We must address the twisted nature we inherited to experience full freedom from its effects.

The clincher is this: satan must operate within the law of God and at God's command. In Job 1, Satan accused Job of only living for God because God made things easy for him, there was a "hedge". God gave satan the power to touch all that Job had but in verse 12 he clearly tells satan that he cannot touch Job himself. Though it may seem the enemy has free reign, he does not. He must obey the authority of God.

SCHEMES OF THE ACCUSER

People in our lives are influenced by the enemy due to hurts, trauma, and false beliefs just as we are. Think of all the times we've had thoughts we knew weren't of God, that didn't originate with us. They were lies of the enemy and for the purposes of this book those lies are known as accusations. II Corinthians 10 tells us this:

> *3 For though we walk in the flesh, we do not war according to the flesh, 4 for the weapons of our warfare are not of the flesh, but divinely powerful for the destruction of fortresses. 5 We are destroying speculations and every lofty thing raised up against the knowledge of God, and we are taking every thought captive to the obedience of Christ, 6 and we are ready to punish all disobedience, whenever your obedience is complete.*

The main tactic of satan is lies. He is the father of lies.[46] The master of deceit is so good that he can appear as an angel of light, as one of truth. Sometimes, satan lies to us and we believe it. If we are not filled with the truth of God, we will fall for his deceit. If we agree with his lies we come out of agreement with God and our disobedience allows us to be imprisoned by the lies. So, not only did we believe the lie, we are experiencing the bondage of our disobedience.

Anyone who recites the accusations of satan agrees with and buys into the lie of the enemy. Agreement with the lies of the enemy creates strongholds (accusations) that keep us bound in thinking and living patterns out of God's will. Arguments and strongholds of the mind are the devices of the enemy, about which we are not to be ignorant!

The good news is that the manifestation of these strongholds (accusations) can be used to our advantage. Once we are aware of the strongholds in our lives, we can apply our operation in the courts of Heaven, the Word of God and the confession of faith to dismantle them. Essentially, we use the Heavenly weapon of our position of authority in the courts of Heaven to address those accusations. And as we address the accusations, we remove their power over us through the blood of Jesus and by the word of our testimony. If someone or something accuses you, it identifies the accusations being spoken by satan himself against in you in court. If he is accusing you here in the earth, he is accusing you before God.

It's a matter of turning those negatives into positives. As we hear accusations from others or the enemy, we take them to court to be judged by God through our covenant with Jesus. Through that covenant the accusations are removed because Jesus already bore the penalty for our disobedience. And, our enemy is forced to be at peace with us on that account because the accusation no longer remains.

Going through this process does not mean that peoples' attitude and actions towards you will always change for the better. However, the obstacles to the blessings that were held up by those accusations are now removed and you are free to receive them and let them take effect in your life!

Time and time again we are encouraged to forgive our brother (Matthew 18:21), make peace with our adversary (Matthew 5:2-25), bless those who curse us (Luke 6:28), and intercede for and restore the lost and broken (Galatians 6:1). We are meant to love and seek the wholeness of people and dwell with our sisters and brothers in peace. But in the realm of the spirit, we can wage war against the arguments and lies brought against us. We must allow God to be our vindicator. When we do this, He not only restores us, but He can also bring light and deliverance to those who are deceived.

---

[40] *Iniquity - The Major Hindrance to Seeing God's Glory Manifested,* Anna Mendez

[41] https://www.blueletterbible.org/lang/lexicon/lexicon.cfm?Strongs=H5771&t=KJV

[42] https://www.blueletterbible.org/lang/lexicon/lexicon.cfm?Strongs=H5753

[43] Mendez, Anna. *Iniquity – The Major Hindrance to Seeing God's Glory Manifested*

[44] https://www.blueletterbible.org/lang/lexicon/lexicon.cfm?Strongs=H6586

[45] https://www.blueletterbible.org/lang/lexicon/lexicon.cfm?Strongs=H2398

[46] John 8:44, https://www.biblegateway.com/passage/?search=john+8%3A44&version=NASB

CHAPTER 7 REVIEW QUESTIONS

1. Who is the accuser of the brethren and what is his purpose in the government of heaven?
2. What is the definition of transgression?
3. How do sins and transgressions lead to iniquity?
4. What is the main scheme of the accuser?
5. What is the main scheme of the accuser?

Chapter 8: The Mediator

In learning to do court cases in the Spirit, one of my first questions was about who was on the legal team. Growing up, I always heard "Jesus is a lawyer in the courtroom" in song lyrics and testimonies that proclaim how Jesus is everything we need. This revelation brought a whole new meaning to that phrase for me. When it comes to mediation, I think everyone has experienced situations in their lives that help to identify with the need for a mediator, especially when dealing with families. These situations can range from silly arguments between children to deep-rooted issues that require legal and/or therapeutic intervention. As kids, my sisters and I regularly required our mother to step in as a mediator. She was always able to bring us to a common ground, a place of compromise and agreement – whether we liked it or not. While this example isn't as weighty as the type of quarrels that require legal mediation, it does display humanity's constant need of mediation.

Typically, in a court setting, you have two opposing sides: the prosecutor and the defense. This is similar in the courts of Heaven, except it is the accuser and the mediator. The purpose of a mediator is to bring two parties together into a place of agreement. This is a legal function, known as a form of alternative dispute resolution. When a dispute is brought into mediation, there is a legal outcome or settlement reached at the end. Additionally, the dictionary lists reconciliation, intervention, intercession and arbitration as synonyms of mediation – all words with significant spiritual context to this subject. Knowing these definitions and how they relate to each other helps to deepen our understanding of mediation.

Reconciliation – to restore to friendship or harmony; to make consistent or congruous; to cause to submit to or accept something difficult[47]

Intervention – to interfere with the outcome or course especially of a condition or process as to prevent harm or improve functioning; divine providence[48]

Intercession – to intervene between parties with a view to reconciling differences; prayer, petition, or entreaty in favor of another[49]

Arbitration – the hearing, settling and determination of a disputed case by a person with power & authority to execute judgment[50]

A mediator is an objective person whose goal is to find common ground and lead each party to a compromise they can agree on. Initially, we may think the mediator is between the enemy and us since those are the two opposing parties, but that is not the case. We are not trying to compromise with the enemy here and God does not desire us to do so. Instead, we are quickly agreeing with his accusations (Matthew 5:25) so that the new covenant can be applied to our lives. According to Hebrews 12:24, Jesus is the mediator of the new covenant. He is also the head of the church, and we, of course, make up the church. It is this combination of Him as the head, and us as the Body of Christ that makes up the mediation team.

Jesus has a number of different roles: He is God, our Lord, our Savior, our Risen King, Jehovah Jireh, the Prince of Peace and the Lord of Lords, etc. This list can go on, as He is an all-powerful, all knowing God for which nothing is impossible. But for this discussion of the mediation team, we will explore five of His roles. When it comes to Jesus being "our lawyer in the court room", it is important to understand Jesus the Mediator, Jesus the High Priest, Jesus the Intercessor, Jesus the Advocate, and Jesus the Head of the Church.

THE FIVE ROLES OF JESUS IN MEDIATION

1. Jesus, our Mediator

"For there is one God and one Mediator between God and men, the Man Christ Jesus." 1 Timothy 2:5

Jesus is the mediator between God and us. He is in a very unique position to be our mediator because of His experience as fully God and fully man. He is completely capable of seeing, knowing and understanding where both parties are coming from. He stands for the demands of God in holiness, while simultaneously standing as man understanding our weaknesses (Hebrews 4:15). My mom was an objective mediator between my sisters and I because her decisions came from the standpoint of all of us being equally her daughters and her desire for what's best for each of us. Jesus, in a perfect way because He's God, is the model for standing objectively in this role. We are all His children; therefore, He wants what is best for us. Simultaneously, He is God; therefore, He wants His will to be accomplished in the earth. In this distinct position, He is perfect to mediate between God and us. From His vantage point, He knows exactly what it will take from each individual for the Kingdom's purpose in the earth to be fulfilled.

"To Jesus the mediator of the new covenant..." Hebrews 12:24a

We've discussed the mediator's role of objectivity for agreement, so now let's go a step further to examine another context of what it means to mediate something. We are moving from the noun to the verb – the act of mediating. Here Jesus is not only a mediator between two parties, but He is also mediating something: the new covenant. To mediate (in this context) is to bring accord out of or to effect by action as an intermediary; to act as an intermediary agent in bringing, effecting or communicating[51]. So, Jesus is standing in the middle, as the go-between, with the new covenant and us. Jesus brings us into the new covenant, helps us to align with it, ensures its effectiveness in us, and communicates every aspect of it for our understanding and application. The finished work of the cross and what Jesus continues to do in Heaven ensures our access to this new covenant.

"But now He has obtained a more excellent ministry, inasmuch as He is also Mediator of a better covenant, which was established on better promises." Hebrews 8:6

"[38] For I am persuaded that neither death nor life, nor angels nor principalities nor powers, nor things present nor things to come, [39] nor height nor depth, nor any other created thing, shall be able to separate us from the love of God which is in Christ Jesus our Lord." Romans 8:38-39

In this role, He works to remove every hindrance and opposing force that would prevent the promises of the new covenant from manifesting in our lives. This is His ministry as the mediator of the new covenant: ensuring that nothing can separate us from obtaining our inheritance in Him. It is a ministry of love that relentlessly labors on our behalf enabling us to walk in everything He purchased on the cross. This ministry includes Jesus' testimony on our behalf based on what His death, burial and resurrection accomplished. This is another legal presentation; as a testimony witnesses, gives evidence and affirms that one has seen, heard or experienced something. It is the foundation of what He presents on our behalf in the courts of Heaven, where testimonies are given.

Revelation 19:10 tells us that Jesus' testimony is the spirit of prophecy. So, His words, which are testifying on our behalf, become prophecy in our mouths in the earth. Prophesying, therefore, is us agreeing with and releasing the testimony of Jesus Christ. When we agree by releasing His testimony, we activate the law of establishing the word, according to 2 Corinthians 13:1. This is another vital place of agreement that allows us to partner with Heaven in order to bring the Kingdom into the earth. As we saw with

Zechariah, prophetic ministry is necessary for us to completely apprehend and receive the fullness of God's will for our lives.

2. Jesus, our High Priest

"[20] *And inasmuch as He was not made priest without an oath [21] (for they have become priests without an oath, but He with an oath by Him who said to Him: 'The Lord has sworn and will not relent, You are a priest forever According to the order of Melchizedek'), [22] by so much more Jesus has become a surety of a better covenant. [23] Also there were many priests, because they were prevented by death from continuing. [24] But He, because He continues forever, has an unchangeable priesthood. [25] Therefore He is also able to save to the uttermost those who come to God through Him, since He always lives to make intercession for them. [26] For such a High Priest was fitting for us, who is holy, harmless, undefiled, separate from sinners, and has become higher than the heavens; [27] who does not need daily, as those high priests, to offer up sacrifices, first for His own sins and then for the people's, for this He did once for all when He offered up Himself. [28] For the law appoints as high priests men who have weakness, but the word of the oath, which came after the law, appoints the Son who has been perfected forever.*" Hebrews 7: 20-28

"[8] *Previously saying, "Sacrifice and offering, burnt offerings, and offerings for sin You did not desire, nor had pleasure in them" (which are offered according to the law), [9] then He said, "Behold, I have come to do Your will, O God." He takes away the first that He may establish the second. [10] By that will we have been sanctified through the offering of the body of Jesus Christ once for all."* Hebrews 10:8-10

As we discussed in the Chapter 6, Jesus Christ's death on the cross was the ultimate fulfillment of the atonement process for us. The high priests of the Old Testament were responsible for carrying out the legal transaction of shedding the blood of animals through sacrifice to pay the debt of the people's sin – death. Jesus, however, not only came as the ultimate sacrifice, but He also came as our high priest. He functions as both the one making the offering and the offering itself. Just as it was with the Old Testament priests, His responsibility is to present an offering that grants God the legal right to show mercy and not judgment towards us. The difference is that He is that offering and has already made the sacrifice, which eliminates the need for continual bloodshed or sacrificing. He was and is perfection. He is qualified to be in the position to cleanse and perfect us despite our weakness and will continue to do so until the Body of Christ reaches perfection. The fact that He was without sin qualified His blood to cleanse us, enabling us to serve the one true living God. It is by taking this pathway, through Him, that He saves us to the "*uttermost*".

When it comes to the concept of "granting God the legal right" to do things, I really had a hard time initially understanding and believing it. Immediately, I thought, "He's God. Why would we have to grant him the right to do anything?" Yet, that thought came from a place of ignorance on my part. I did not understand what it actually took to get God's will accomplished in the earth along with the opposition present to stop this from happening. This is one of the reasons we discussed both concepts of dominion and co-laboring earlier in this book. God gave us dominion in the earth; therefore, everything He does here happens through us, His people. We partner with God (co-labor) to bring His will into the earth. Because God cannot lie, and His word cannot return to Him void, He is not going to ever violate Himself, as He is His word. Even our choices to give up our dominion to the enemy don't cause God to go back on His word. They do, however, tie His hands, because again, He will never violate His word. The wages of sin are death (Romans 6:23). Because that is the law of the Lord, only the following can reverse this penalty:

1. Jesus' death, burial & resurrection – His blood.
2. We must accept Jesus as our Lord & Savior to receive this salvation.
3. His blood must be applied to every area of our lives.

So, we have Jesus' sacrifice as the perfect resolution for all, yet He is still acting as our high priest? Yes, because of the fact that all He did has yet to be fully appropriated and manifested in the earth through our lives. So as our high priest, He helps us get to this place. His "*eternal and unchangeable priesthood*" tells us that He will remain in this place to ensure His blood is applied to every area of our lives. Thereby, fully establishing the new covenant in the earth and achieving His original intent of Kingdom dominion in the earth. This is the legal responsibility that Jesus carries out as our High Priest. It is an even greater responsibility and role than that of the Old Testament high priests. The Old Testament High Priest was an actual type and shadow of Jesus Himself, meaning they represented something (Jesus) that was to come.

"The law is only a shadow of the good things that are coming-not the realities themselves. For this reason it can never, by the same sacrifices repeated endlessly year after year, make perfect those who draw near to worship. If it could, would they not have stopped being offered?" Hebrews 10:1-2

He is still in the place of mediation, standing between God and man, in this role as High Priest. Through His sacrifice, He ensures that the penalty of sin (death) is not applied to our lives, which grants God the legal right to reconcile our lives once again. Any un-yielded, un-confronted areas in our lives standing in opposition to the will of God are a result of sin, iniquity and transgression. As we discussed in the previous chapter, in some cases this is from our own choices and in others, it is from our bloodline. However, in each of these instances, we must take on the responsibility of addressing and applying the blood of Jesus to it to experience full deliverance. When these things are present in our lives, satan has a legal right to use them against us and this ties God's hands, as it is His law that established these principles. God is holy, and He still hates sin, Jesus' sacrifice didn't change this fact. So, Jesus as our high priest removes the legal penalties applicable to our lives (because of sin), thus giving God free reign to bless us and establish His will in our lives. His blood is "*cleansing our conscience from dead works*" enabling and allowing us "*to serve the living God.*"

"[11] *But Christ came as High Priest of the good things to come, with the greater and more perfect tabernacle not made with hands, that is, not of this creation.* [12] *Not with the blood of goats and calves, but with His own blood He entered the Most Holy Place once for all, having obtained eternal redemption.* [13] *For if the blood of bulls and goats and the ashes of a heifer, sprinkling the unclean, sanctifies for the purifying of the flesh,* [14] *how much more shall the blood of Christ, who through the eternal Spirit offered Himself without spot to God, cleanse your conscience from dead works to serve the living God?* [15] *And for this reason He is the Mediator of the new covenant, by means of death, for the redemption of the transgressions under the first covenant, that those who are called may receive the promise of the eternal inheritance.*"
Hebrews 9:11-15

"[14] *Seeing then that we have a great High Priest who has passed through the heavens, Jesus the Son of God, let us hold fast our confession.* [15] *For we do not have a High Priest who cannot sympathize with our weaknesses, but was in all points tempted as we are, yet without sin.* [16] *Let us therefore come boldly to the throne of grace, that we may obtain mercy and find grace to help in time of need.*" Hebrews 4:15-16

His perfect life on earth opened the door for us to not only come to the throne of God, but to BOLDLY come to the throne of God. We now have the privilege of obtaining grace and mercy directly from the throne of God. This is another place where we should stop and take note of a supernatural shift that took place with the new covenant: The tearing of the veil opened the holiest place to us – the Holy of Holies – a place that previously had restricted access. This is our doorway to operating in heavenly realms while on earth. Jesus is the door, He is the way for us walk in a supernatural life.

"[16] For indeed He does not give aid to angels, but He does give aid to the seed of Abraham. [17] Therefore, in all things He had to be made like His brethren, that He might be a merciful and faithful High Priest in things pertaining to God, to make propitiation for the sins of the people. [18] For in that He Himself has suffered, being tempted, He is able to aid those who are tempted." Hebrews 2:16-18

In His humanity, Jesus identifies with our humanity. It causes Him to be the best High Priest for us, merciful and faithful. His ability to identify with our humanity allows Him to provide the help we most need. He is empowered to assist us perfectly. Having been where we are and experienced what we're experiencing, He is quite capable of executing his office as High Priest to give us what we need to achieve all things pertaining to God.

"[11] And every priest stands ministering daily and offering repeatedly the same sacrifices, which can never take away sins. [12] But this Man, after He had offered one sacrifice for sins forever, sat down at the right hand of God, [13] from that time waiting till His enemies are made His footstool. [14] For by one offering He has perfected forever those who are being sanctified." Hebrews 10:11-14

3. Jesus, our Intercessor

"Therefore He is also able to save to the uttermost those who come to God through Him, since He always lives to make intercession for them." Hebrews 7:25

"Who is he who condemns? It is Christ who died, and furthermore is also risen, who is even at the right hand of God, who also makes intercession for us." Romans 8:34

Jesus is the ultimate intercessor! He doesn't just intercede for us sometimes, He LIVES to do it always. He is constantly making intercession for us without fail. He is the epitome of praying without ceasing; and being our intercessor is a demonstration of His saving power.

In that being our intercessor enables Him to save us completely (*to the uttermost*) because He never ceases to intercede on our behalf. An intercessor is one who intervenes on behalf of another, especially by prayer. They stand in the gap, as a bridge, between two parties for the purpose of reconciling their differences.

Of course, this role has legal implications as well. This is a strategy that grants God the legal right to intervene in a situation. There are many examples in the Bible of an intercessor who petitioned the Lord to intervene in a situation, successfully turning the judgment of God into mercy. Abraham and Lot are one of my favorite examples of this truth. Lot wasn't praying for his own deliverance; in fact, he was enjoying his sinful state and had no idea the consequences he would pay for the actions committed in sin. However, Abraham petitioned God for mercy repeatedly until there was a resolution, saving Lot and his family. Please note that Abraham petitioned God to intervene. You see, God gave us all free will. He will not step into our situations without permission, request or the pleading (interceding) of another human on our behalf. This is one aspect that makes intercession such a powerful skill.

"May the Lord answer you in the day of trouble; May the name of the God of Jacob defend you; [2] May He send you help from the sanctuary, and strengthen you out of Zion; [3] May He remember all your offerings, and accept your burnt sacrifice. Selah [4] May He grant you according to your heart's desire, and fulfill all your purpose. [5] We will rejoice in your salvation, and in the name of our God we will set up our banners!
May the Lord fulfill all your petitions." Psalm 20:1-5

"*I, even I, am He who blots out your transgressions for My own sake; and I will not remember your sins. [26] Put Me in remembrance; Let us contend together; State your case, that you may be acquitted."* Isaiah 43:25-26

Biblically, intercession has always required an offering or sacrifice, which puts God in remembrance of us along with His promises to us. A wonderful example of this principle is in 2 Samuel 24:10-25, in which David insists on paying for his own threshing floor, refusing to offer anything to God for which he has not paid. The Lord sent a plague to Israel due to David's sin. Here you can see God's law of the penalty of death for sin in action. After seeing the result of the plague, David petitioned the Lord to save the people. God responded by telling David to build Him an altar. After David paid and made the burnt offering sacrifice, the scripture says that God heeded David's prayers and the plague was withdrawn.

This occurrence perfectly displays how it wasn't solely David's prayer that caused God to answer, but it was the combination of his petition along with his sacrifice. God, in turn, responded to his sacrifice and petition by saving the people. However, there is even more to this situation. One of the most significant parts of this is the fact that before David was grieved by the amount of people killed and made his petition to save the rest; the Lord was grieved by their deaths first. Verse 16 says that the Lord relented and told the angel to stop. It is at this moment, AFTER God told the angel to withdraw his hand, that David sees the angel and petitioned the Lord. So we can clearly see here that God desired to stop the consequences of His own law. Nevertheless, He did not actually remove the angel and the plague from the people until David's request along with his completed sacrifice. This is a major key, depicting the importance of intercession and how it grants God the opening into the earth to legally intervene. This is also why we must take our own roles as intercessors very seriously.

How powerful is it to have God Himself in this role for us?! AMAZING!! Jesus' own body and blood are the offering on which He bases His intercession (Hebrews 7:25-27). Which means His intercession is in full agreement with the testimony of His blood and sacrifice.

4. Jesus, our Advocate

"My little children, these things I write to you, so that you may not sin. And if anyone sins, we have an Advocate with the Father, Jesus Christ the righteous. [2] And He Himself is the propitiation for our sins, and not for ours only but also for the whole world."
1 John 2:1-2

"For You, Lord, are good, and ready to forgive, and abundant in mercy to all those who call upon You." Psalm 86:5

Jesus is our advocate with the Father. This means He speaks in favor of, supports, pleads, and urges on our behalf to the Father. This is very similar to the role of intercessor, one that petitions the Lord on behalf of someone else. Legally speaking, an advocate is an individual who counsels, gives legal advice, presents and argues another's case and pleads the cause of someone else in court[52]. In many cultures, advocates and lawyers are professionally one in the same. Lawyers advocate for their clients by representing their client's best interests. Advocates are valued because they are often the voice, defender and the representative of their client; promoting the issues that are important to them that affect their daily lives. This role is especially important for those who are vulnerable and unable to advocate for themselves.

"*Open your mouth for the speechless, in the cause of all who are appointed to die. [9] Open your mouth, judge righteously, and plead the cause of the poor and needy."* Proverbs 31:8-9

"But He saves the needy from the sword, from the mouth of the mighty, and from their hand. [16] So the poor have hope, and injustice shuts her mouth." Job 5:15-16

Being an advocate for others is a biblical principle and an attribute of God. It is commanded and exhibited by Him and His people throughout the Old and New

Testaments (Isaiah 1:17, Jeremiah 22:3, 2 Corinthians 8:13-15). Jesus completely fulfilled the old covenant and made way for the new covenant; in this regard, He became our advocate. He advocates for us in the courts of Heaven, before the throne of God, and to the Father. We learn from 2 Corinthians 5:21 that through Jesus we can become the righteousness of God. Him imputing His righteousness on us allows us to stand before our Holy God. It allows us to stand in court before the throne like Jesus does.

5. Jesus, the Head of the Church

"That the God of our Lord Jesus Christ, the Father of glory, may give to you the spirit of wisdom and revelation in the knowledge of Him, [18] the eyes of your understanding being enlightened; that you may know what is the hope of His calling, what are the riches of the glory of His inheritance in the saints, [19] and what is the exceeding greatness of His power toward us who believe, according to the working of His mighty power [20] which He worked in Christ when He raised Him from the dead and seated Him at His right hand in the heavenly places, [21] far above all principality and power and might and dominion, and every name that is named, not only in this age but also in that which is to come. [22] And He put all things under His feet, and gave Him to be head over all things to the church, [23] which is His body, the fullness of Him who fills all in all." Ephesians 1:17-23

"For the husband is head of the wife, as also Christ is head of the church; and He is the Savior of the body" Ephesians 5:23

Jesus is the Head of His Church; it is His body. His headship speaks to the authority and direction of God in Christ and how He relates to us as His body. In a natural sense, the body is inoperable without its head. There is no life without a head. It houses the brain – the powerhouse – and is the place from where all directives are sent and processed. This truth applies to Jesus Christ as the head; He is the life of His body (John 14:6). When we receive salvation, accepting Jesus as our Lord and Savior, we receive the ability to come into communion with Him and the fullness of the Godhead. Having Him as our head immediately brings us into unity with Him. Ephesians 1 gives us a list of benefits we have as the saints, which all come by way of Jesus Christ. He is our inheritance.

Our unity with Christ as our head gives us access to all things that are in Him and everything that can be done through Him. We have access to each of these roles because we are in Christ, seated with Him in heavenly places (Ephesians 2:6). Specifically, Christ as our head brings a greater depth to our connection to each of His legal roles that we've discussed. Where He is, we are, also. Thus, as Jesus is seated and operating in heavenly realms, we are, too. As He is present before the throne of God, in the courts of Heaven, we have this same access, too.

"*And He is before all things, and in Him all things consist.* [18] *And He is the head of the body, the church, who is the beginning, the firstborn from the dead, that in all things He may have the preeminence.* [19] *For it pleased the Father that in Him all the fullness should dwell,* [20] *and by Him to reconcile all things to Himself, by Him, whether things on earth or things in heaven, having made peace through the blood of His cross.*" Colossians 1:17-20

• • •

These (brief) descriptions of only five of the roles of Jesus Christ give us just a glimpse of the magnitude and AWE-someness of the nature of the one true living God. Here we can really begin to grasp the fact that we have GOD Himself going to GOD Himself on our behalf. WE CANNOT LOSE! While we are discussing the roles of Jesus in His mediation between the Father and us, we must not lose sight of the oneness of God. The Lord, our God, is one (Deuteronomy 6:4, Ephesians 4:4-6). There is no disagreement amongst the Godhead; division is completely against the nature of God. He is the embodiment of unity; through all of His diverse roles, manifestations, expressions, characteristics, etc., He never ceases to be one God, in complete unity with Himself.

"For in Him dwells all the fullness of the Godhead bodily; [10] and you are complete in Him, who is the head of all principality and power." Colossians 2:9-10

His oneness is a benefit for us, which ensures our victory. We are not talking about a situation where God the Father is against us and Jesus is for us. Jesus doesn't have to argue a case for us to be found innocent in the same way lawyers do for judges on earth. Jesus only does what He sees His Father doing. Our Father already desires our deliverance, salvation, freedom, and the fullness of His will to be made manifest in our lives. He desires all men to be saved and come to the knowledge of the truth (1 Timothy 2:4). Yet, Jesus is the only way to make this possible, as no one comes to the Father except by Him (John 14:6). It is through Jesus that we receive forgiveness, salvation, and access to the Father and heavenly realms. Because of Him, when God looks at us He sees His son, His blood and His righteousness. Through our understanding of these roles, we can see all of the saving work of Christ come to fruition in our individual lives and in the earth.

"Lord, you are my lawyer! Plead my case! For you have redeemed my life. [59] You have seen the wrong they have done to me, Lord. Be my judge, and prove me right." Lamentations 3:58-59

---

[47] Merriam-Webster Online, https://www.merriam-webster.com/dictionary/reconcile
[48] Merriam-Webster Online, https://www.merriam-webster.com/dictionary/intervention
[49] Merriam-Webster Online, https://www.merriam-webster.com/dictionary/intervention
[50] Merriam-Webster Online, https://www.merriam-webster.com/dictionary/arbitration
[51] Merriam-Webster Online, https://www.merriam-webster.com/dictionary/mediate
[52] Dictionary Online, http://www.dictionary.com/browse/advocate

CHAPTER 8 REVIEW QUESTIONS

1. What are the two opposing sides in the courts of Heaven?
2. Who is our mediator? Define this role.
3. Name two ways this role is fulfilled.
4. What was the ultimate fulfillment of atonement for us?
5. What 5 roles does Jesus play in mediation?

Chapter 9: The Mediation Team

So, where do we come in? We come in alongside Jesus on the mediation team as the church (His Body!). Since dominion was originally given to and intended for us on the earth, we play an essential role in ensuring that the full dominion of the Kingdom happens here. Everything that God wants to do in the earth, He does through us, the humans. That is why it is vital for us to co-labor with the fullness of the Godhead. In partnering with God, learning Him and His will intimately, we are empowered and authorized to use our dominion in the earth to bring forth His Kingdom.

THE ROLE OF THE CHURCH (BODY OF CHRIST)

It is easy to hear the word church and think about the traditional experiences of gathering with other believers in a building. Based on these experiences, it would seem that the definition of church is a place that one attend on Sundays, with other people of like mind, certain terminology and language in repetition, along with the services, programs and events that take place. However, this is not the truth of God. Our realities have not been in complete alignment with who the church is ordained to be biblically. The Body of Christ's purpose is much greater than our experiences have made it out to be. Operating in the governmental dominion of the Kingdom is the essence of who we are called to be as the church. The Greek word for the church is ekklēsia/ecclēsia: it literally means called out ones[53]. It is used to refer to a council; an assembly of people convened at the public place of the council for the purpose of deliberating. Several of the words used in this definition have legal implications.

Council – a body of persons specifically designated or selected to act in an advisory, administrative or legislative capacity; an executive or legislative body assisting the governor; an ecclesiastical assembly[54]

Deliberate – a careful consideration before making a decision; the process by which the outcome of a case is determined[55]

In the next few paragraphs, we are going to discuss historical facts of ecclēsias. The term ecclēsia was used in ancient Greece (Athens specifically). The ecclēsia was the public legislative assembly of the Athenians. It was the dominant, popular political council of their democracy[56]. The government required the candidate to be a citizen of Athens in order for them to qualify to join their assembly. According to the Encyclopedia Britannica, this council had all political power including functioning in judicial proceedings and the administration of the law[4]. Some of the assembly's legal responsibilities included:

- Nominating and electing magistrates and other officials
- Determining legislation and voting on proposals of law
- Voting on decrees and treaties
- Declaring war and developing military strategy
- Final control over policy
- Conferring special privileges on individuals[4]

We can see similarities here to functions of the branches of government in the United States. While that is not an exhaustive list of the Athenian Ecclēsia's duties, it is enough to paint a picture of their legal authority, governance and rulership. They were not known for when they gathered, where they gathered, or the special experiences they had at their gatherings; they were known as a governmental ruling body that carried significant weight and authority in their region. This is significant to our understanding of our identity as the Body of Christ. We should be known for having substantial governmental authority to establish the Kingdom of God in the earth.

The Sanhedrin is another example of an ecclēsia of that time, having a closer relationship to the Body of Christ because of its religious nature. The Sanhedrin was the supreme Jewish legislative and judicial court. It is comparable to a supreme court in the United States. It was an assembly of 23 or 71 rabbis (judges) that were appointed to sit as a tribunal in every city in ancient Israel[57]. This assembly legislated all aspects of Jewish religious and political life within the parameters laid down by biblical and rabbinic tradition. Their responsibilities included:

- Sole ability to try the king
- All questions of the law were put to them for final decisions
- Declarations of war
- Extending the boundaries of the temple & Jerusalem
- Issuing enactments and decrees with respect to the applicability or release from legal requirements
- Determining the penalty for breaking the law[5]

The Pharisees and Sadducees were part of this assembly along with the high priest. It was the Sanhedrin who took up the conspiracy to have Jesus crucified.

"57 Those who had arrested Jesus took him to Caiaphas the high priest, where the teachers of the law and the elders had assembled. 58 But Peter followed him at a distance, right up to the courtyard of the high priest. He entered and sat down with the guards to see the outcome. 59 The chief priests and the whole Sanhedrin were looking for false evidence against Jesus so that they could put him to death. 60 But they did not find any, though many false witnesses came forward. Finally two came forward 61 and declared, "This fellow said, 'I am able to destroy the temple of God and rebuild it in three days.'" 62 Then the high priest stood up and said to Jesus, "Are you not going to answer? What is this testimony that these men are bringing against you?" 63 But Jesus remained silent. The high priest said to him, "I charge you under oath by the living God: Tell us if you are the Messiah, the

Son of God." 64 *"You have said so," Jesus replied. "But I say to all of you: From now on you*
will see the Son of Man sitting at the right hand of the Mighty One and coming on the
clouds of heaven."
65 *Then the high priest tore his clothes and said, "He has spoken blasphemy! Why do we*
need any more witnesses? Look, now you have heard the blasphemy. 66 *What do you*
think?", "He is worthy of death," they answered. 67 *Then they spit in his face and struck him*
with their fists. Others slapped him." Matthew 26:57-67

It was also the place where Paul's trial was held in Acts 23:1-11:

"Paul looked straight at the Sanhedrin and said, "My brothers, I have fulfilled my duty to
God in all good conscience to this day." 2 *At this the high priest Ananias ordered those*
standing near Paul to strike him on the mouth. 3 *Then Paul said to him, "God will strike you,*
you whitewashed wall! You sit there to judge me according to the law, yet you yourself
violate the law by commanding that I be struck!" 4 *Those who were standing near Paul*
said, "How dare you insult God's high priest!" 5 *Paul replied, "Brothers, I did not realize that*
he was the high priest; for it is written: 'Do not speak evil about the ruler of your people.'"
6 *Then Paul, knowing that some of them were Sadducees and the others Pharisees, called*
out in the Sanhedrin, "My brothers, I am a Pharisee, descended from Pharisees. I stand on
trial because of the hope of the resurrection of the dead." 7 *When he said this, a dispute*
broke out between the Pharisees and the Sadducees, and the assembly was
divided. 8 *(The Sadducees say that there is no resurrection, and that there are neither*
angels nor spirits, but the Pharisees believe all these things.) 9 *There was a great uproar,*
and some of the teachers of the law who were Pharisees stood up and argued vigorously.
"We find nothing wrong with this man," they said. "What if a spirit or an angel has spoken
to him?" 10 *The dispute became so violent that the commander was afraid Paul would be*
torn to pieces by them. He ordered the troops to go down and take him away from them by
force and bring him into the barracks.

[11] The following night the Lord stood near Paul and said, "Take courage! As you have testified about me in Jerusalem, so you must also testify in Rome."

As we can see with both examples, the Sanhedrin had the authority to find people worthy of death if they determined a law was broken.

Given the historical context of an ecclēsia, we are now able to recognize that Jesus' and the apostles' use of the word for the church was a direct reference to a governmental ruling body. In those days, everyone who heard the terminology would have immediately recognized its significance. Culturally, without prior knowledge of Greek or Hebrew tradition, as Westernized Christians, this is not an easy fact for us to discern. This reality indicates why governments during that time found the church along with the apostles so offensive. They were considered a threat to them because it was government vs. government in their eyes. The government of the church was affecting the power and economy of these regional governments. The apostles were doing an excellent job of bringing the Kingdom into the earth through the name of Jesus Christ. They established the laws and the ways of the Kingdom so that it had dominion in those regions. This is, effectively, how the apostles received the reputation of turning the world upside down. They were persecuted so heavily because of this Kingdom dominance as well. And so should be the reputation of the modern-day church; we should be known for turning the world upside down.

"Now when they had passed through Amphipolis and Apollonia, they came
to Thessalonica, where there was a synagogue of the Jews. [2] Then Paul, as his custom
was, went in to them, and for three Sabbaths reasoned with them from the
Scriptures, [3] explaining and demonstrating that the Christ had to suffer and rise again from
the dead, and saying, 'This Jesus whom I preach to you is the Christ.' [4] And some of them
were persuaded; and a great multitude of the devout Greeks, and not a few of the leading
women, joined Paul and Silas. [5] But the Jews who were not persuaded, becoming envious,

took some of the evil men from the marketplace, and gathering a mob, set all the city in an uproar and attacked the house of Jason, and sought to bring them out to the people. [6] *But when they did not find them, they dragged Jason and some brethren to the rulers of the city, crying out, "These who have turned the world upside down have come here too.* [7] *Jason has harbored them, and these are all acting contrary to the decrees of Caesar, saying there is another king—Jesus."* [8] *And they troubled the crowd and the rulers of the city when they heard these things."*
Acts 17:1-8

Now, what is the one common requirement shared in becoming a part of the early ecclēsia and a United States president? Drum roll please... Citizenship! This was always a determining factor in a person's ability to be a part of these governing bodies. It is our salvation through Jesus Christ that gives us citizenship in the Kingdom. As citizens of the Kingdom, we are called to gather together (Hebrews 10:25) and operate as collectives in our local ecclēsias, which make up the whole Body of Christ. Ecclēsia is used 118 times in the New Testament. While the majority of those times, it is translated as church; there are three times it is used in reference to a legal assembly of believers. We find these examples in Acts 19 during the riot at Ephesus:

"And when Paul wanted to go in to the people, the disciples would not allow him. [31] *Then some of the officials of Asia, who were his friends, sent to him pleading that he would not venture into the theater.* [32] *Some therefore cried one thing and some another, for the assembly was confused, and most of them did not know why they had come together.* [33] *And they drew Alexander out of the multitude, the Jews putting him forward. And Alexander motioned with his hand, and wanted to make his defense to the people.* [34] *But when they found out that he was a Jew, all with one voice cried out for about two hours, "Great is Diana of the Ephesians!"* [35] *And when the city clerk had quieted the crowd, he said: "Men of Ephesus, what man is there who does not know that the city of the Ephesians is temple guardian of the great goddess Diana, and of the image which fell*

down from Zeus? [36] *Therefore, since these things cannot be denied, you ought to be quiet and do nothing rashly.* [37] *For you have brought these men here who are neither robbers of temples nor blasphemers of your goddess.* [38] *Therefore, if Demetrius and his fellow craftsmen have a case against anyone, the courts are open and there are proconsuls. Let them bring charges against one another.* [39] *But if you have any other inquiry to make, it shall be determined in the lawful assembly.* [40] *For we are in danger of being called in question for today's uproar, there being no reason which we may give to account for this disorderly gathering."* [41] *And when he had said these things, he dismissed the assembly."* Acts 19:30-41

Repeatedly throughout the New Testament, we see the church as an assembly and gathering of believers. It is never referred to as just one person. It is impossible for one person to be an assembly, council or governmental ruling body by himself or herself. Accordingly, we make up the church, but we cannot be the church on our own (Romans 12:4-5). We are individually the temples of the Holy Spirit and we are not our own (1 Corinthians 6:19). Collectively, our temples form the Body of Christ, His bride, and the church.

As the ecclēsia of God, we have legal responsibilities just as any other ecclēsia has in the past. Here are a few examples outlined in scripture:

1. Binding and Loosing

"And I also say to you that you are Peter, and on this rock I will build My church, and the gates of Hades shall not prevail against it. [19] *And I will give you the keys of the kingdom of heaven, and whatever you bind on earth will be bound in heaven, and whatever you loose on earth will be loosed in heaven."* Matthew 16:18-19

This is a pretty popular scripture for many believers. We often quote it, discuss it, pray it and command the things in our lives working against us to be bound. Still, we rarely have the depth of full understanding of what these words mean and how we should apply them to our individual lives or corporately as a body. Because of this, we are regularly operating at a very superficial level when it comes to spiritual warfare, and living beneath our privileges as Sons of God.

Bind – to impose definite legal obligations or duties upon a person or party to an agreement; indicates an agreement has been consciously made and certain actions are now either required or prohibited with a contract or judgment[58].

Loose – to set free from bonds; to release from or dissolve existing legal obligations or duties

While aspects of these definitions can be found on Google, digging into the Greek words used in this scripture allows us to recognize that these words have legal characterizations as well. We can also see that from other scriptural references.

"No one can enter a strong man's house and plunder his goods, unless he first binds the strong man. And then he will plunder his house." Mark 3:27

"And ought not this woman, being a daughter of Abraham, whom Satan hath bound, lo, these eighteen years, be loosed from this bond on the sabbath day?" Luke 13:16

"Whom God hath raised up, having loosed the pains of death: because it was not possible that he should be held by it" Acts 2:24

We want to not only declare spiritual forces be bound, but also to create legal parameters that demand they stay bound. It ensures that our declarations have legal decrees (authoritative, governmental orders that have the force of law, and judicial decision) as their foundation. Binding and loosing is part of our judicial responsibilities as the ecclēsia of the Most High God. It is a process we begin in the courts of Heaven. This is a two-fold responsibility, in that there are aspects that must be taken care for the advancement of the Kingdom of God as well as for the deterioration of the kingdom of darkness. We must establish legally binding contracts that allow God the legal right to transform and impact the earth, while simultaneously legally dissolving (loosing) contracts that have given the enemy legal right to the earth. This works both on a corporate and individual level. We receive much more power in handling both aspects of this, verses just one or the other. Once we establish this legislation in heaven, our prayers have the backing of heaven and the foundation of God's judgments to stand on in a whole new way. Every believer, especially intercessors, should learn to wield this responsibility skillfully.

2. Royal Priesthood

"You also, as living stones, are being built up a spiritual house, a holy priesthood, to offer up spiritual sacrifices acceptable to God through Jesus Christ." 1 Peter 2:5

We have discussed the importance of the role of the priest and its legal characteristics through Jesus Christ. It is a role that applies to us as His body as well. Although we no longer make ceremonial sacrifices using the blood of animals, we are still called to make sacrifices in our everyday lives. Peter referred to them as "*spiritual sacrifices*". We are called to live a sacrificial life, which includes offering our own bodies as living sacrifices to God (Romans 12:1). Sacrifices are not easy or enjoyable; they are akin to death. They require the relinquishing of something valuable in order to be valid. For us, it is our lives, our wills, our fleshy desires and the tendencies in us that go against the nature of God. We cannot become a holy priesthood, acceptable to stand before our holy God, without dying to our flesh first (Romans 8:13). When Jesus tells us, we must deny ourselves and take up our cross to follow Him (Matthew 16:24-27), He gives instructions on living as a holy priesthood, worthy of the call on our lives. We are called to follow the model that Jesus set for us: dying to achieve the will of the Father.

"But you are a chosen generation, a royal priesthood, a holy nation, His own special people, that you may proclaim the praises of Him who called you out of darkness into His marvelous light." 1 Peter 2:9

In living this way, both being and making sacrifices, we become sanctified, consecrated vessels hallowed out for the exclusive use of God. Holy vessels are essential for bringing the dominion of the Kingdom of God into the earth. We, as holy vessels, are fundamental for co-laboring with the Lord to bring forth His will. This is a legal position for us to stand in. Like with the sacrifices of the Old Testament and Jesus' sacrifice, our sacrifices grant God legal rights in the earth as well. A consecrated, sanctified lifestyle of holiness positions us in a place of intimacy with our God, enabling us to know His will and legally establish it in the earth the way He desires.

3. Ambassadors for Christ

"Now then, we are ambassadors for Christ, as though God were pleading through us: we implore you on Christ's behalf, be reconciled to God." 2 Corinthians 5:20

Every believer wants to be an ambassador for Christ, right?! It is a wonderful, Godly goal, which we should all desire to attain. Nonetheless, what does it actually mean to be an ambassador? Historically, an ambassador has always been a governmental position. It is a diplomatic official of the highest rank, sent by one sovereign or government to another as its resident representative[59]. This person has the authority to represent and conduct the business of the government or king who sent them. In fact, we find examples of this exact position throughout the Old Testament. They can be seen doing the biding of their governments in Numbers 20:14, 21:21, Judges 11:7-19, Joshua 9:4, 1 Kings 20:2-6, 2 Kings 14:8, 16:7, 18:14, and 2 Chronicles 32:31.

"And for me, that utterance may be given to me, that I may open my mouth boldly to make known the mystery of the gospel, [20] for which I am an ambassador in chains; that in it I may speak boldly, as I ought to speak." Ephesians 6:19-20

Paul says we are ambassadors for the mystery of the gospel – the teachings and life of Jesus Christ. Therefore, we are ambassadors for the government of the Kingdom of God! The highest government in existence has chosen us, as its ecclēsia, to be its ambassadors. Amazing! Hence, it is our responsibility to represent and conduct the business of the only wise God. We do this by carrying out his principles, decrees, declarations, and establishing his law in the earth.

4. His Witnesses

"But you shall receive power when the Holy Spirit has come upon you; and you shall be witnesses to Me in Jerusalem, and in all Judea and Samaria, and to the end of the earth." Acts 1:8

In this day and age, it is easy to find a Christian caught up in a heated debate, attempting to defend the word of God. It is something that people take pride in, especially on social media. Yet, God never called or even asked us to defend Him. He is His word and He needs no defense, particularly not from His own creation. He did, however, call us to be His witnesses. A witness is someone who sees something take place, and then gives evidence and testimony as to what exactly happened. Their testimony can become a legal declaration of what they have experienced. Witnesses are integral to proving anything legally; whether someone is innocent or guilty, there is always some kind of witness to prove that point. We, as the Body of Christ, are to be witnesses of the gospel of Jesus

Christ to the whole earth! Jesus tells us that it is through the power of the Holy Spirit that we are able to do so.

"Then he said, 'The God of our fathers has chosen you that you should know His will, and see the Just One, and hear the voice of His mouth. [15] *For you will be His witness to all men of what you have seen and heard."* Acts 22:14-15

We have a powerful testimony as members of the ecclēsia of Jesus Christ. Our shared testimony gives us fellowship with each other and with the Godhead (1 John 1:2-3). Our light – the way that we live our lives for God – is a testimony to the people around us of the goodness of the Father (Matthew 5:14-16). Testifying of Jesus causes Him to testify of us in heaven (Matthew 10:32). It is also through our testimony that we overcome the enemy (Revelation 12:11). Our testimony is valuable in heaven and in earth, both naturally and spiritually. So being a witness for God furthers His Kingdom while simultaneously overcoming the kingdom of darkness.

• • •

The combination of Jesus' roles and our roles as His ecclēsia creates a team that cannot lose. This is why we like to call the mediation team: Team Victory! The victory is already ours. It is ordained as so by the will of God. However, we must take our roles and fulfill our responsibilities on the team in order to bring the Kingdom of God into the earth the way He desires. Legal duties must be established in legal places, i.e. the courts of Heaven are our foundation for establishing legalities in Heaven to bring into the earth. Let us all take our place and learn to rule and reign with our God!

"Therefore I endure all things for the sake of the elect, that they also may obtain the salvation which is in Christ Jesus with eternal glory. [11] *This is a faithful saying: For if we died with Him, We shall also live with Him.* [12] *If we endure, We shall also reign with Him. If*

we deny Him, He also will deny us. [13] *If we are faithless, He remains faithful; He cannot deny Himself."* 2 Timothy 2:10-13

---

[53] Strong, LL. D. S.T.D., James. The New Strong's Expanded Exhaustive Concordance of the Bible. G1577, page 81
[54] Dictionary Online, http://www.dictionary.com/browse/council
[55] Merriam-Webster Online, https://www.merriam-webster.com/dictionary/deliberate
[56] Encyclopedia Britannica Online, https://www.britannica.com/topic/Ecclesia-ancient-Greek-assembly
[57] Encyclopedia Britannica Online, https://www.britannica.com/topic/sanhedrin
[58] The Law Dictionary Online, https://thelawdictionary.org/bind/
[59] Bible Study Tools Online, https://www.biblestudytools.com/dictionary/ambassador/

CHAPTER 9 REVIEW QUESTIONS

1. What is the Greek word for church? Define this word.
2. Which two historical councils during Biblical times were discussed in a similar context as the church?
3. Why is it important to understand the legal aspects of binding and loosing?
4. For what are we ambassadors? What makes this role governmental?
5. Name two more responsibilities of the church as an ecclesia.

SECTION III: THE ANATOMY OF THE COURTS OF HEAVEN QUIZ

1.) What is the definition of prayer?

____

____

____

2.) Prayer first takes place... (Please pick one answer)

a. In our hearts
b. The property of the church
c. In our homes
d. In the Court Room of Heaven

3.) Why is it important to get backing from the Courts of Heaven?

____

____

____

4.) Please explain the ways that the blood of Jesus testifies our behalf in the Courts of Heaven?

____

____

____

5.) The accuser of the brethren is ... (Please pick one answer)

a. The Backslider
b. Your neighbor
c. satan
d. The third of the angels that fell with satan

6.) Please explain the difference between sin, iniquity and transgression.

____

____

____

____

7.) According to scripture, how often does the accuser bring accusations against us in court? (Please pick one answer)

a. Every morning
b. On the Sabbath
c. At midnight
d. Day and Night

8.) Please explain the role of the Mediator in the Courts of Heaven?

____
____
____

9.) An ekklēsia is
e. a council or assembly of the called out ones
f. a study of the book of Ecclesiastes
g. A Psalm, Hymn and spiritual song
h. a binding contract

10.) What is the purpose of an ekklēsia?

____
____
____

11.) Please explain function of the ekklēsia.

____
____
____

Glossary of Terms

This glossary is created to provide understanding of the meaning of phrases and terms used throughout this book. The definitions in this glossary are meant to give clarity to the manner in which said terms are used in the context of this book. Some definitions are not based on a general understanding of the words, rather their applications to the Government of Heaven.

Accusation: *a charge or claim of wrongdoing.*

accuser: *the accuser is satan. He is the one responsible for accusing man of violating the laws of God and enforcing punishment for violation of those laws.*

Ambassador: *a diplomatic official of the highest rank, sent by one sovereign or government to another as its official representative; this person has the authority to represent and conduct the business of the government or king who sent them*

Angel: *a being created by God to serve His purposes and minister to God's people.*

Arbitration: *the hearing, settling and determination of a disputed case by a person with power & authority to execute judgment*

Atonement: *the satisfaction or reparation for a wrong or injury; to make amends, reconciliation or agreement; a legal transaction.*

Believer: *a person who has accepted Jesus Christ as Messiah and has been born again into the family and kingdom of God.*

Bind: *to impose definite legal obligations or duties upon a person or party to an agreement; indicates an agreement has been consciously made and certain actions are now either required or prohibited with a contract or judgment.*

Cloud of Witnesses: *a phrase used to describe the assembly of the Body of Christ in Heaven who bear witness before God of the happenings on earth and serve the purposes of God in heaven.*

Co-laborer: *a term used to describe a Christian who lives in his or her inheritance as a child of God and works with God to accomplish His will and establish the reign of His kingdom on earth.*

Council: *a body of persons specifically designated or selected to act in an advisory, administrative or legislative capacity; an executive or legislative body assisting the governor; an ecclesiastical assembly*

Court Case: *a judicial proceeding in the courts of heaven through which one intercedes to request petitions for people, places, and entities in accordance with God's will and addresses accusations and evidence that prevent God's will from happening in the earth.*

Courts of Heaven: *The courts of Heaven are a Part of the Kingdom's Heavenly governmental system.*

Declaration: *a positive, explicit, or formal statement; a proclamation*

Decree: *authoritative, governmental orders that have the force of law, also a judicial decision*

Deliberate: *a careful consideration before making a decision; the process by which the outcome of a case is determined*

Dominion: *the power or right of governing control. Sovereignty and the right of rulership over a territory or people group. Regarding the Believer, it is a place of ruling over the inheritance given to one by God in a manner consistent with the precepts and way of Kingdom of God.*

Ekklēsia/ecclēsia: *the Greek word for church. It means called out ones; an assembly of the people convened at the public place of the council for the purpose of deliberating.*

Flesh: *the carnal, unredeemed nature of man. The flesh is embodies the desires, proclivities and actions of man that are not of God.*

God's General: *phrase indicative of someone who has a high rank in the Kingdom of God, along with the authority and leadership that cause them to bring the Kingdom of God into the Earth. Roberts Liardon, who spent a significant portion of his life researching these types of people, coined the term "God's General."*

Godhead: *the mysterious nature of the One, Triune God – Father, Jesus and Holy Spirit.*

High Priest: *one of the names and roles of Jesus; used to describe HIs role as both the one making sacrifices and the sacrifice itself before God for mankind. In the Old Testament, the high priest was responsible for making sacrifices to atone for the people's sin, which released the mercy of God.*

Iniquity: *the seed and wicked DNA that is passed down in the bloodline; the twisted, perverted evil nature imparted to each person at birth – sets the whole pattern of ungodliness*

Intercession: *to intervene between parties with a view to reconciling differences; prayer, petition, or entreaty in favor of another*

Intervention: *to interfere with the outcome or course especially of a condition or process as to prevent harm or improve functioning; Divine providence*

Kingdom of God: *a phrase used to describe the realm of dominion and rulership of God. The kingdom of God is not just a location. It is any place where a person, group, or territory is subject to and submitted to the rulership of God.*

Language of Tongues: *the supernatural language given to believers who receive the indwelling of the Holy Spirit with evidence. This supernatural language is the Holy Spirit praying through the believer and is used to pray the exact and perfect will of God. There are various types of tongues described throughout the New Testament. We also refer to this gift as praying in tongues, or praying in one's heavenly language.*

Loose: *to set free from bonds; to release from or dissolve existing legal obligations or duties*

Mandate: *a commission given by God to accomplish a particular task or to fulfill a role in His kingdom.*

Mediator: *one of the names and roles of Jesus; used to describe His role not only as the one who mediates between God and man but also as the one who mediates the new covenant to believers through His death, burial and resurrection.*

Mina: *an ancient unit of weight and value equal to one-sixtieth of a talent*

Petition: *a formally drawn request that is addressed to a person (or people) in authority or power, soliciting some favor, right, mercy or other benefit; an application for a court order or for some judicial action; basic definition of prayer*

Reconciliation: *to restore to friendship or harmony; to make consistent or congruous; to cause to submit to or accept something difficult*

Revelator: *a believer who, through a life of consecration and pursuit of God and His word, receives revelation of mysteries from God regarding His Word, His Will and His Dominion.*

satan: *the former angel who fell from heaven and became the adversary of God. satan rules the evil kingdom of darkness and contends against God's children to prevent the kingdom of God from being established in the earth and to prevent God's children from living their destinies.*

Scroll: *a written document of heaven that states God's will, purpose and judgment regarding a particular matter. Each person, place and entity created by God has a scroll that details God original intent and plan for that person, place or entity.*

Sin: *the perverted desire of the heart; the thought and intent against the laws of God.*

Son of God: *the identity of a believer. In accepting Christ as one's Savior, one is born of the spirit and into the family of God.*

Sonship: *the position of authority of each believer in Christ. Sonship refers to knowing one's identity, authority and responsibilities as a child of God.*

The Spirit: *The Spirit is Holy Spirit, who is God. He is the Spirit of Truth, the Comforter, the Leader and Guider into all truth, the One who was sent to us after Jesus' ascension and indwells man upon receiving His baptism.*

Transgression: *a violation of the law, an offense or infringement; willful acts of disobedience and infractions against God*

Verdict: *a statement of decision made to settle a dispute in a court of law.*

ANSWER KEY

SECTION I: DOMINION

Chapter 1: Introduction to the Government of Heaven

1. Supreme authority over a land/territory
3. Psalm 139:8, Exodus 19:4-5, John 3:16
5. Man was cursed, lost access to God

Chapter 2: The Kingdom of Heaven

1. Heaven is His throne and the earth is His footstool.
3. Full of Life - (Revelation 21:4), Wealthy - (Philippians 4:19), Rejoices & Celebrates (Revelation 19: 6-7), A Sin Free Zone - (Matthew 13: 41), Complete Healing & Restoration - (Revelation 22:2), Has a Government - (Isaiah 9:6)
4. The blood of Jesus gave us access and opened up the Heavens for us to be rejoined back to the father.

Chapter 3: Holy Spirit, The Key to Our Supernatural Life

1. Made in God's image - the Godhead, Body, Spirit, Soul
3. The edification process encompasses the steps needed to build a spiritual superstructure in order for us to house the anointing, the power and the operations of God. This is when God can fully trust us with Kingdom responsibility.
5. Prayer, Scriptures, Fasting, Consecration, Worship/Intimacy

SECTION II: CO-LABORERS

Chapter 4: Being Co-Laborers with Christ

1. That his servants would use the money he gave them to manage and increase his business fairs while he was away and
3. To have intimate fellowship and relationship
5. To take dominion in the earth and establish God's Kingdom

Chapter 5: Generals in the Kingdom

1. A person who has a high rank in the Kingdom of God, along with the authority and leadership that cause them to bring the Kingdom of God into the Earth.
3. The baptism of the Holy Spirit with the evidence of speaking in tongues.
5. She was a woman of faith and carrier of the presence of God.

SECTION III: THE ANATOMY OF THE COURTS OF HEAVEN

Chapter 6: Introduction to the Courts of Heaven

1. The basic definition of prayer is a petition unto God. A petition is defined as a formally drawn request that is addressed to a person (or people) in authority or power, soliciting some favor, right, mercy or other benefit; it is an application for a court order or for some judicial action.
2. Jesus places prayer in the courtroom in the parable of the wide and the judge. The widow is very persistent in seeking the judge for justice until he finally gives it to her.
3. Because he saw Him who is invisible.

Chapter 7: The Role of the accuser

1. Satan is the accuser and his purpose is to draw a clear distinction between what is and is not of God.
3. To commit an act of sin due to rebellion against the command of God.
5. To present lies and truth and entice us to believe them so that we act on the lie and disobey God.

Chapter 8: The Mediator

1. The mediator and the accuser.
3. Jesus is the mediator between God and us & Jesus mediates the New Covenant for us.
4. Jesus' death on the cross.

Chapter 9: The Mediation Team:

1. Ekklēsia/ecclēsia. It literally means called out ones. It is used to refer to a council; an assembly of people convened at the public place of the council for the purpose of deliberating.
3. Athenian Ecclēsia & Sanhedrin
5. Paul says we are ambassadors for the mystery of the gospel. This person has the authority to represent and conduct the business of the government or king who sent them.